DATE			

A Student's Guide to Conducting Social Science Research

Barbara Benedict Bunker

Howard B. Pearlson

Justin W. Schulz

HUMAN SCIENCES PRESS
A Division of Behavioral Publications, Inc.

New York

Library of Congress Catalog Number 74-11814

ISBN: 0-87705-238-7 paperback
0-87705-236-0 hardcover

Printed in the United States of America
56789 987654321

LIBRARY OF CONGRESS CATALOGING
IN PUBLICATION DATA

Bunker, Barbara Benedict.
    A student's guide to conducting social science research.

    1. Social science research. I. Pearlson, Howard B.,
joint author. II. Schulz, Justin W., joint author. III. Title.
H62.B84   300'.7'2   74-11814

CONTENTS

ABOUT THE AUTHORS

Barbara Benedict Bunker
is a social psychologist in
the Department of Psy-
chology at the State Uni-
versity of New York at
Buffalo. Howard Pearlson
and Justin Schulz are Re-
search and Teaching Assis-
tants in Psychology at the
State University of New
York at Buffalo. The re-
sponsibility for writing
this manuscript was shared
equally by the authors and,
therefore, their names appear alphabetically.

NOTE TO STUDENTS

This research guide is intended to supplement and enrich your social science course. Those of you who have taken science courses are familiar with the one or two periods a week spent in biology, physics, or chemistry labs. This guide may be viewed as a laboratory component of social studies. The following pages will provide you with first-hand experience in the methods by which social scientists (psychologists, sociologists, political scientists, economists, and anthropologists) probe the issues of the human experience that they decide to investigate.

The guide is divided into three sections. The first section provides an overview of the methods by which social scientists conduct research. The second section provides a detailed account of two studies which are the work of social scientists. The third section provides you, the student, with the opportunity to engage in activities that are typical of social science research. References are provided for those who wish to go on to more sophisticated material. You can use it as a guide to understanding research or as a step-by-step guide for a project of your own. We have tried to make this guide understandable and interesting. We hope you will enjoy using it.

part I

research guide

Satisfaction of one's curiosity is one of the greatest sources of happiness in life.

Linus Pauling

A lot of people have the idea that research is a very dry academic activity that developed in the ivory towers of universities. They do not think it has much to do with their day to day lives.

Our idea is just the opposite. We believe that most people are engaged in informal processes which are similar to those of professional social science researchers.

We all make observations about other people every day and we use the regularities we observe in the social world as a basis for our action. For example, a girl who is dating one boy can get to know his habits quite well. After a few dates she has probably observed that if he says he will pick her up at 7 p.m., he will (a) be there early, (b) be there within a few minutes of seven, (c) be there ten to fifteen minutes after seven, or (d) call about 7:10 to say he got tied up and won't be there until 7:30. From the experience of actually observing his behavior she can eventually predict what he is likely to do. Being able to predict what he will do is very useful. It allows her to get ready early if he is an early arriver or to take her time if he consistently shows up late.

Take a minute to think about how this process works in your own classroom. Most students are careful observers of their teachers' behavior and in time they can predict quite accurately what their teachers are about to do or say. Are there some areas where you can make accurate predictions about your teacher? Check with other students; do they agree? What data (observations) do you use?

When we compare the everyday activities of most people with the work of social scientists, we do not really find much difference. We all try to (a) describe events; (b) explain what causes these events; (c) predict the future occurrence of these events; and (d) learn how to control these events to our own advantage. The main differences are that the scientist uses systematic methods and considers objective evidence (that is, evidence which anyone can check) rather than subjective opinions or the word of an authority.

The subjective idea (opinion) has its place in the scientific process. The best of scientists rely upon hunch, intuition, and plain old curiosity in guiding their work. However, personal opinion is used only as a starting point for developing ideas. Objective facts, "evidence," produce the final verdict on whether or not ideas are supported.

What we are saying is that science is a way of checking your ideas about how the world works, of testing them to see if they hold up. In this guide we will cover some of the rules that you can use to do research. The methods outlined here will show you how to draw conclusions based upon objective evidence, for in science it is only through objective evidence that we can be certain of what we know.

The reason scientists undertake research investigations is that they have noticed something interesting in the world around them and have decided to find out more about it. Their basic motivation is their curiosity and the hope that they will make interesting and useful discoveries. You may know the story of Sir Alexander Fleming, who noticed some green mold in a dish in which he was trying to grow a bacteria culture. He became interested in the growth of the mold and what it did to the bacteria. That spark of interest led to the discovery of penicillin.

Of course research does not always lead to discoveries of the magnitude of penicillin. What it does do, however, is provide a disciplined method for thinking about problems and understanding our world more fully.

In everyday life, people often have ideas which could be pursued as research if they wanted to investigate their ideas more carefully. These ideas usually come from noticing events and their relation to other events. For example, you may have heard another student make one of the following observations:

> "The good teachers in this school are really interested in the students";
>
> or
>
> "Parents who order their kids not to use drugs are more likely to have kids who try drugs than those who let their kids make their own decision";
>
> or
>
> "Girls can't get elected to important offices in this school."

Each of these statements is an observation about a relationship between two factors. They may or may not be accurate observations. In the form in which we have presented them, these are assertions based on one person's view of the world. In order to find out if they are correct, they could be stated as hypotheses and a method developed to test them. And that would be scientific research—taking a personal, subjective impression and testing it with objective evidence.

We have prepared this research guide to better acquaint you with the steps involved in developing and conducting a research project. This will permit you to investigate your own questions. Although no two research projects are identical, there are general steps that most people developing a research project follow. In this guide we will present descriptions of the steps and illustrations of their applications.

The steps that we will be referring to are these:

1. Deciding what to investigate
2. Formulating hypotheses or exploratory questions
3. Selecting a method
4. Developing your research design
5. Training in the selected method

6. Collecting data
7. Drawing conclusions from your data
8. Writing up what you have done
9. Planning further research

REFERENCES   Hyman, Ray. *The Nature of Psychological Inquiry.* En-
glewood Cliffs, N.J.: Prentice-Hall, 1964.

McCain, G. and Segal, E. *The Game of Science.* Belmont,
Calif.: Brooks/Cole, 1969.

Scott, N. A. and Wertheimer, M. *Introduction to Psychological Research.* New York: John Wiley, 1962.

DECIDING WHAT TO INVESTIGATE

The first step in any scientific investigation is to decide
what topic interests you and, more specifically, what aspects of the topic you wish to investigate. It is important to be as specific as possible about the aspects of the
topic you wish to investigate.

We stress the need to be specific for two reasons:
First, the more specific you are, the easier it will be to
plan your project since you will be more certain of the
questions for which you will be seeking answers in your
investigation. Secondly, research projects take time to
conduct, involve a great deal of work, and cost money.
Since researchers are limited in the number of hours
they can devote to a research project, the number of
people available to carry out the investigation, and the
amount of money they can afford to spend, they cannot
possibly investigate every aspect of their topic in any
one research project. Specificity helps you to focus
on what can be completed with the time and energy
available.

FORMULATING HYPOTHESES OR EXPLORATORY QUESTIONS

One way to be sure you are being very specific is to put your ideas in the form of hypotheses or exploratory questions. Stating hypotheses increases our exactness by specifying what we expect to find. It directs our attention towards specific things that we might overlook, were we not paying attention to them before we started. As an example, assume we are watching people at a three-day rock concert. Without any predictions about what to expect, we are not sure of what to look for—so we try to look at everything. In our efforts we note how people dress, whether they are alone or in groups, who goes where; in short, we try to get as much information as possible. The amount of information we could possibly collect is enormous. Thus, since we cannot cover everything, there is a good chance we will fail to see something important.

Now let us return to the rock concert, but this time we will make a prediction. We predict that the crowd will be more interested in Dr. John The Night Tripper than in Chicago. We can observe now how people behave toward both groups and we are better able to make a comparison of the effects of the two groups on audiences because our attention is directed to a specific activity that we think is important. Our prediction has told us to look at one behavior (interest in a particular group) rather than at everything.

Before starting our research then, we should spend time thinking about what we expect to find. Thinking about the problem, we will try to make predictions that are as specific as possible. These specific predictions are called *hypotheses*. But sometimes we are not able to make exact predictions; then we rely on developing *exploratory questions.* When we are unable to develop predictions, exploratory questions can still give some direction to our efforts. Often we use exploratory questions to get some insight about a phenomenon and then develop hypotheses from the answers to our questions. The predictions can then be tested in subsequent research.

Looking at the prediction we have made in this example, it appears we have a problem: How do we get people to agree on what "interest" is? How can we know if one group is more interesting than another? If science is to be public, then we need a definition that anyone can use. To solve this problem, we use an *operational definition* for concepts such as "interest." We define these ideas not by what a person experiences directly but by some behaviors which can be observed by anyone.

Rather than argue about what constitutes interest in a group (or what a person experiences when "interested" in something), we will choose to define it by a behavior which is public: interest in a rock group can be measured by the number of newly released albums sold for each group during the concert at the record concession tent. We can actually measure the number of new releases sold for the first group and the number of new albums sold for the second group. And by our definition of interest we will know which group is more interesting to the audience.

Of course we could have chosen to define interest in some other way, such as by people's reporting how interested they felt. The researcher simply chooses the definition that he thinks best represents what he wants to study. In this case we have chosen the number of albums sold as the definition of interest because we assumed 1) people will not buy a new release if it does not interest them, and 2) self-reports could be unreliable, as trying to interview a representative sample of the audience could be extremely difficult in such a large, disorganized crowd.

We hope it is clear now that in doing research we need *hypotheses* (predictions) or at least *exploratory questions* (what should we look for), and *operational definitions* of concepts. In addition, we also try to *measure* what we are studying. (Recall that we counted the number of albums sold for each group.) With numbers we can tell whether one group is greater than another. Are there more male or female students in your school? You could ask people for their impressions, but they could easily be wrong. To be exact, we count the number of school records marked male and the number marked female. We determine if people show more interest in one rock group than another by counting the sales of new releases. Observing without measuring can be very unreliable, so we try to measure as exactly as possible.

SELECTING A METHOD

The next step is to select the most appropriate method to test your ideas. In this section, we will acquaint you with the advantages and disadvantages of three approaches to social science research: the survey, observation, and the experiment. Later sections will discuss these methods in more detail.

SURVEY

In the survey approach, subjects are asked to answer a number of questions pertaining to the research interests of the investigator. There are two variants to this approach: the questionnaire, in which subjects are asked to fill out answers to a prepared series of questions, and the interview, in which they are verbally questioned by an interviewer who records their comments and answers.

The survey is the preferred method if the researcher wishes to obtain a large amount of information from a large number of subjects.* However, it is only applicable when the researcher's questions can be answered by questionnaire-type data. Thus, a survey would be appropriate for finding out the political preferences of voters residing in different areas of the state. The researcher would simply ask the voters for whom they intended to vote. In other instances, for example, studying the reactions of subjects to competitive situations, the survey would be less appropriate. Subjects might not be aware of how they respond to competition. In addition, they might not wish to tell the researcher their "true" feelings on the matter.

If the researcher deems the survey appropriate, he is still faced with the problem of whether to conduct an interview or employ a questionnaire. Each has its advantages. The questionnaire is easy to administer and should be employed when the researcher asks straightforward questions. The interview is more time-consuming and costly to administer. However, it allows the researcher to ask more complicated questions. The interviewer can clarify problems the respondent might have in answering particular questions.

OBSERVATION   Observation is possibly the least used of the three methods. In this approach, the researcher simply observes what occurs naturally. The researcher can either determine beforehand the content of his observations, e.g., comparing specific behavior in two different classrooms, or observe things in a more random manner, e.g., trekking around the wilds of the Amazon or Manhattan to observe whatever might occur in a particular tribal culture.

---

*Surveys vary from as large as several thousand subjects to less than one hundred, depending on the sampling procedure and complexity of the topic.

This approach has the disadvantage of not providing the researcher with full control over the situation. It is, however, a useful technique for gathering information, especially if experimentation might have some negative effect on the subjects. For example, suppose a researcher was interested in the effects that lack of affection and love have on infant personality development. He would not be justified in experimentally depriving infants of maternal affection since it might be damaging. Research that might harm people psychologically is never justified. However, he could observe the manner in which infants and their natural mothers relate to each other in their own homes. After making a number of observations of mothers and their infants, he might be able to observe differences between infants whose mothers are very loving and affectionate and those whose mothers are not.

EXPERIMENT

The experiment is a situation in which the researcher can exercise much more control over the selection of subjects, the assignment of subjects to treatment groups, and the content of the treatment administered. Experiments are conducted either in laboratories or in natural settings, such as school, business, or even street corners.

Sometimes researchers do not wish to grow old and gray waiting for the proper conditions to occur, so they create conditions and assign subjects to experimental groups. Suppose, for example, a researcher wants to find out the extent to which student performance is influenced by the competitiveness in a test-taking situation. He could wait until a particular test is administered under both relaxed and competitive conditions and compare the results, but that might take a long time. He could, however, create the two conditions in an experiment. He could test one group of subjects in a situation where the test instructions are read in a stern, competitive manner, and compare their performance to that of a similar group tested in a relaxed, casual manner.

By controlling both the assignment and treatment of subjects, the experimenter is no longer studying events as they naturally occur in the "real world." Although the experiment may have the disadvantage of being somewhat artificial and contrived, the experimenter assumes that the increased control allows him to clearly answer his research questions and more than offsets the disadvantage posed by the artificiality of the experimental situation.

ETHICAL ISSUES   In conducting research, you should always remember that you are dealing with human beings, not machines. You are therefore responsible for the experience subjects have in your research project. The following rules of thumb should be followed:

1. Do not subject persons to any treatment you would not want to receive yourself.
2. Use as little deception as possible in conducting your research.
3. Always debrief subjects after conducting your research. That is, subjects should be given the opportunity to learn why they participated. They should be given the opportunity to learn the purpose, predictions, and results of your study.
4. Keep all information confidential. Research is not an excuse to be nosy. Do not ask subjects "personal" questions that are not pertinent to your study.

REFERENCES Kelman, Herbert C. *A Time to Speak: On Human Values and Social Research.* San Francisco: Jossey-Bass, 1968.

Surgeon General's directives on human experimentation. *American Psychologist,* 1967, 22:350-355.

DEVELOPING YOUR RESEARCH DESIGN

Suppose you were about to design a study. How can you decide if the study you are planning is worthwhile? For one thing, you would want your results to be clear and meaningful. For another, you would want your study to be applicable to the real world. Finally, you would probably want your results to be both stable and reproducible.

Each of these issues is a separate criterion against which you can evaluate the study you are proposing. In scientific terms, we refer to the first criterion as *internal validity*, which answers the question "Is this study going to produce clear results?" The second is *external validity*, and it answers the question "Will the results be relevant to other situations?" The third is *reliability*, and it answers the question "If we did this study again with a different group of subjects, would we get the same results?" In the following paragraphs each issue will be discussed in turn.

INTERNAL VALIDITY

The most important requirement of a good study is that it permit clear and precise interpretation of results. The study should be designed (set up or planned) in such a way that the researcher can determine what factors account for his results. If the study is set up such that the researcher cannot interpret the cause of his results, time and energy will have been expended fruitlessly. Here is an example:

Let's assume you want to determine whether Sesame Street improves the reading ability of second grade students. You want to design an internally valid study that will:

> 1. tell you whether reading scores improve as a result of watching Sesame Street;

2. clearly determine what specific factors are responsible for any improvement in reading scores
that might be found.

How would you go about doing this?

One approach you could use is to give a reading
test to a group of first graders who had watched Sesame
Street since the beginning of the school year. If these
students score above the national average on the reading
test, could you unambiguously infer that the effectiveness of Sesame Street has been demonstrated? In other
words, could you conclude that your results are internally valid? The answer is "Most certainly not!" because several other explanations could account for these results.
(You may want to go back to the description of the Sesame Street experiment and try to figure out what the
other explanations could be before you read further.)

One alternative explanation would be that the
reading scores improved because as time passed and the
children got older their reading capacity improved. Perhaps they would have improved even if they had not
watched Sesame Street. Another explanation would be
that these children did not improve at all. Perhaps they
were good readers to begin with. Unless you had a measure of their reading scores earlier in the school year, you
couldn't tell if the scores changed.

A more internally valid approach would be to as-
sess the reading level of a group of students both before
and after watching Sesame Street. Reading level could
be measured both in September and in January. Using
this approach, one could definitely tell if there was an
improvement in reading scores for these subjects. However, we would still not be able to tell whether the effects were due to Sesame Street. (Think again why not!)
The possibility would still exist that the student's reading scores would have improved as a function of the
mere passage of time. After all, they would be six months
older (and presumably more experienced) on the second
reading test.

We could make the experiment still more internally valid by using what is known as a *control group.* That is, we could select another group of students of approximately equal reading ability and have them not watch any television programs. If the group watching Sesame Street improves more in reading, we would have a pretty good idea that the T.V. watching was responsible.

Does this make our inference that Sesame Street was responsible for the improved reading score internally valid? Well, almost, but not quite. There would still be the possibility that watching any television rather than the content of the specific program watched (in this case, Sesame Street) was responsible for the results. We could eliminate this possibility by creating a second control group that watches another T.V. program, e.g., Bugs Bunny, instead of Sesame Street. If television alone is responsible for the improvement in reading scores, then the Bugs Bunny and Sesame Street groups should both improve more in reading than the no television control group. However, if the content of the particular program is responsible, the Sesame Street group should improve more than both the Bugs Bunny group and the no television group.

We have just covered an important research principle. In order to have an internally valid experiment, you must control all factors that could account for the results. You can do this by setting up a control group for *each* factor you wish to consider. A control group is similar to the original treatment group in all respects except for that factor. If the two groups show different results you will know that the particular factor on which they differed is responsible.

Figure 1 illustrates exactly what was done to the three groups in our hypothetical (make-believe) experiment. The experimental group, shown in Row 1 was given a reading test at Time 1 (during September), watched Sesame Street until January, and was given a second reading test at Time 2 (during January). Control group 2 (shown in Row 2) was also given a reading test in September, but they were not allowed to watch T.V. between September and January. As with the experimental group, they were retested in January. Finally, control group 2 was tested in September and watched Bugs Bunny periodically until January, at which time their reading scores were retested.

Groups	Pretreatment Measurement	Treatment	Post-treatment Measurement
Experimental Group	Reading Test Time 1	Sesame Street	Reading Test Time 2
Control Group 1 (Controls for time effect)	Reading Test Time 1	No T.V.	Reading Test Time 2
Control Group 2 (Controls for general television effect)	Reading Test Time 1	Bugs Bunny	Reading Test Time 2
	September		January

Figure 1: Design for the Sesame Street Experiment

In review, we made certain that there was an improvement in reading scores by measuring students both before and after they had been directed to watch the Sesame Street program. We controlled for the possibility that the results could be due to the mere passage of time by observing the reading improvements of a group not exposed to T.V. Finally, we controlled for the possibility that the results could be due to T.V. *per se* rather than a particular program by having a second control group watch Bugs Bunny. The fact that the treatment group improves more than the no T.V. control group would indicate that T.V. watching is responsible for the results. The fact that the treatment group improves more than the Bugs Bunny control group would indicate that the particular content of the program—in this case, the content of Sesame Street—is responsible for the improvement in reading.

EXTERNAL VALIDITY

In the previous section, we have demonstrated how to design a study so that the results are clear. The next problem is how to select subjects similar to the people you wish to understand. Essentially, what you want to do is to take one or more small groups of people, study something about their behavior, and then apply the findings to larger populations of people. By carefully selecting the small groups to be studied, we are better able to generalize our results to others.

Let's say we wished to generalize the results of our Sesame Street study. We would have to include subjects who are typical of the mainstream of first grade students. If we included only the students with the highest IQ scores and found that Sesame Street improved their reading scores, we would not be able to conclude that these results were applicable to average or below average students. Similarly, if Sesame Street failed to improve the reading scores of below average students, we could not safely conclude that the results would be applicable to average or above average students.

One way to handle this problem would be to select subjects from a class having children with all levels of I Q. From this class we could then generate a *random* list of subjects for participation in the study. That is, we could select subjects such that every member of the class has an equal chance of being chosen. If such procedures are followed, we should end up with a "representative sample," that is a small group of children with a range of I Q very much like the range in the general population of first graders. We would then be in a position to confidently state that the results of our study are applicable to most first grade students.

Let's pursue this point a bit further. Suppose we wanted to select a representative sample of fifteen first graders and place five of them in the experimental group, five in control group 1, and five in control group 2 (see Figure 1 on page 23). For starters, we could choose a class that has a representative group with regard to I Q.

The next problem would be how to select the fifteen subjects. One strategy might be to select volunteers. However, this could create problems. People who volunteer might be different from those who do not. A second approach might be to assign persons from the front row to the experimental group and persons from the back rows to the control groups. Once again however, we run into the same problem. Persons who sit in the front may somehow be different from persons who sit in the back. We don't know that for sure, but the only way to avoid that possibility would be to select our sample by a random method. If we placed the names of all students in a hat and drew fifteen names, each child would have an equal chance of being selected and we would have a *random sample.* The first five names would be assigned to the experimental group, the next five to control group 1, and the last five to control group 2.

> ### ACTIVITY
>
> You might wish to take a random sample from your own class. Let's say you wanted a sample of eight students. Have someone put separate slips of paper in a hat— representing the names of all the students in your class. Have another person draw eight names. This will result in an unbiased selection of students. You probably will have students selected who sit in all sections of the room and are representatively divided according to sex, race, class standing, and other factors.

RELIABILITY   One more problem remains, that of determining the degree to which results are stable and reliable. If another group of subjects could be studied in a similar experiment and if the same results are obtained, we would have added confidence that the previous findings are stable and reliable. Since you will probably be doing only one study, reliability will be less important to you than the other two criteria.

Backstrom, C. H. and Hursh, G. D. *Survey Research.*   **REFERENCES**
    Evanston, Ill.: Northwestern University Press, 1963.
Campbell, D. L. and Stanley, J. C. *Experimental and
    Quasi-experimental Designs for Research.* Chicago:
    Rand McNally, 1970.
Rosenthal, R. On the social psychology of the psycho-
    logical experiment: The experimenter's hypothesis as
    unintended determinant of experimental results.
    American Scientist, 1963, 51:268-283.

TRAINING IN
THE SELECTED METHOD

The next step in your research can be a lot of fun. During this phase you will have a chance to prepare and practice for the period of real data collection. In research this is the time when you test things out, make adjustments in your method, etc. Once you start the data collection, however, no changing is allowed. You don't stop, you don't look back, you just collect the data as rapidly and as accurately as you can. It's similar to tuning up a car engine. While the mechanic is tuning up the engine he may tinker with a lot of things, make adjustments, and try out a variety of adjustments to improve its running, but once he gives the keys back to the owner and the owner drives away, that's all the adjustments there can be.

       Since different methods require different kinds of tune-ups, we will discuss the three major ones separately. They are the survey, which is done either with a questionnaire (paper and pencil form) or a personal interview, observation, and the experiment.

THE SURVEY
(Questionnaire)

When you are planning your study, you will develop a set of questions which you will present to the people in your study. These questions will be printed on a form of a page or more which you will ask the people in your study to fill out and return to you.

Questionnaires are "administered" in a variety of ways. Sometimes they are filled out in one place, such as a classroom, and everyone completes them at the same time. In other cases, they are mailed out and returned by mail. It's also possible that people are approached in person and asked to participate in a survey. Perhaps this has happened to you while shopping or on the highway when you were stopped for a traffic survey. Whatever the situation, it is important that the printed form be titled so that everyone will know what the survey is about and who is doing it. Following the title, brief but clear directions are given about how to fill out the form. For example, a heading might look like this:

MAGAZINE READERS SURVEY

This survey has been planned by the junior class council to find out what types of magazines are being read by high school students. The survey will be used to recommend to the library that they subscribe to some new magazines.

Please indicate your class: ___Freshman ___Junior
                           ___Sophomore ___Senior

I am a: ___female ___male

Below is a list of magazines. Please check all that you read and circle to the right the number that indicates how often you read them.

	Regularly	*Most of the time*	Occasionally
___*People*	1	2	3
___*Field and Stream*	1	2	3
___*Seventeen*	1	2	3
___*Newsweek*	1	2	3

What questions will you ask? The content will be determined by the purpose of your survey. In addition, you will need to be careful about how you ask the questions. It is very easy to ask questions in such a way that the person responding believes that you want him to give you a particular answer. For example, suppose someone asked you, "Do you believe that young people should be allowed to purchase things as dangerous to their health as alcohol or cigarettes?" Would you feel that this was an objective question and that the researcher didn't care what answer you gave? Questions should always be phrased so that whatever your own opinion is, it doesn't show in the question. That way your respondent will answer what he really thinks, not what he thinks you want him to say. The technical term for the problem we are discussing is *bias*. There are all kinds of ways that bias can creep into a research project. That doesn't mean that the researcher doesn't have his own opinions or hope that the research will show a particular conclusion. Of course he does, but he tries to keep that opinion out of the research project itself.

A second question you will have to settle is the form of the questions you use in your questionnaire. There are two major forms which you will recognize from your experience with examinations. They are the fixed choice question (multiple choice) or the open-ended question (short answer essay). Each kind has advantages and disadvantages. The fixed choice question is one in which you pose a question and the person responding has to select from a group of answers the one he prefers. (Remember, in research, unlike exams, there is no "right" answer, only some alternatives.) For example, suppose the following question was asked:

CHOICE QUESTION
"Have you ever used marijuana?"
1. No, never
2. I tried it once
3. I smoke it once in a while
4. I smoke it several times a month
5. I smoke it pretty often

Here is another way to ask the same question:

SCALE QUESTION

How much marijuana do you smoke?
(check the box that is most like you)

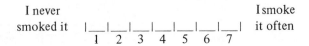

A third type of question about the same general topic might look like this:

RANK ORDER QUESTION

Listed below are five drugs used by some students in high school. Put a "1" by the drug you use most frequently, put a "2" in front of the drug you use next most frequently, and so on until you have ranked all five drugs.

___ aspirin

___ alcohol

___ marijuana

___ pep pills (amphetamines)

___ downers

Now let's look at the advantages and disadvantages of these three types of question, the choice question, the scale question, and the rank order question. Look again at the first example, the choice question, and read it over carefully. Now imagine you had used marijuana on weekends for a period of about six months and then quit completely. At the time of the question-

naire you had not smoked marijuana for a year. Which
answer would you pick? Do you see the problem? The
most accurate answer for you isn't in the list of responses to pick from. That means if you do pick one, it won't
be a really valid description of your behavior. For that
reason, it is important to include in the responses to
fixed questions most of the possible answers. How do
you know what they are? Usually researchers try to
check on this by trying the questionnaire out on some
people and getting their reactions. This is called "pilot
testing."

Choice questions have a variety of forms. The
example above gives the most common forms. Sometimes you may want to ask the respondent to select all
of the responses that are true for him instead of just
one. The question you ask will usually help determine
what form the answer takes.

Now let's look at the scale question. It appears
that whatever your experience with marijuana you could
find a place to check on the scale. Then, when the data
is tabulated you can assign a number to each box (usually 1 is low and 7 is high) and compute scores for each
group of people. For example, you could compare the
scores of boys and girls or of seniors and sophomores.
When you want to make comparisons, the scale question
has an advantage in that it gives you a numerical score
for each person. However, it doesn't give you as precise
information as the choice question. The rank order question will provide information about the order of importance of a number of items in relation to each other. So
you see that different types of questions yield different
information. The type of question you choose depends
on what information you decide you need for testing
your ideas.

In general, the biggest advantage of fixed choice
questions is that when you get your data back you can
count up the answers and know what your results are
pretty fast. It is more work in the beginning to make up

really good fixed choice questions, but it is less work at the end analyzing the results.

Open-ended questions are just the reverse. They don't take as long to formulate because all you do is ask a question, e.g., "Have you ever smoked marijuana?" and then the person filling out your questionnaire writes in his own answer. The problem comes when you get back all those answers, and you have to "code" them. You have to read them and develop a set of categories, then have some "judges" read them and decide into which category they fall. The details of this procedure are beyond the scope of this book, but it takes considerable time to do it accurately. That is why we recommend that if you have selected the questionnaire method, most of your questions should be of the fixed response type. If you do find open-ended questions useful, we would suggest that you include them at the end of the survey after the fixed choice questions.

After you have an instrument which you think you'd like to use, you will want to "pilot test" it. This means finding a few people like those who will be in your final testing population and asking them to fill it out. If you are going to administer it to students in your school, it's best to try it out with students from another high school like yours. If you are going to go out into the community, test it in another area of town that is similar to the one you'll use in your project. *Never* use the same people in a pilot test and then again in the research itself. (Can you think why?)

When you pilot test, work with one person at a time. After the person has filled in the questionnaire you will want to go over it with him making some notes to yourself of his responses. Here are some examples of some questions which you might want to ask.

1. What was it like filling out this questionnaire?
2. Were there any questions with which you had difficulty? That you didn't understand?
3. Was it either interesting or boring? Too long? Or short?

Then, go through the questionnaire *one question at a time* and be sure that the person understood the question the way you intended it to be understood. You will be surprised how easy it is to write a question you were sure was clear and then find someone with a completely different interpretation of what the question is asking! You will probably want to try your questionnaire out on ten to fifteen people. From these interviews you will be able to revise your questionnaire and improve it, i.e., you will "get the bugs out" of your questionnaire.

Finally, if you select a questionnaire you will have to decide how to administer it. Will you give each one individually? If you do, each person who administers it should introduce the form the same way. You may want to practice giving instructions on what it's about, who you are, who is sponsoring the project, and what they should do. The same issues apply if you administer it in groups. In addition, you need to be sure there is a comfortable place to write and that people don't discuss the form until they have finished filling it out.

THE SURVEY (Interview)

The interview is a conversation conducted by a researcher with someone else who has the information needed to answer the researcher's questions. Like questionnaire surveys, interviews are conducted in all kinds of places. You may have been stopped in your car to answer some questions about traffic. Perhaps at an airport or shopping mall someone asked you to take five minutes to answer a few questions. Sometimes people may have asked to come into your home for an extensive interview of an hour or more.

Whatever the situation, the interviewer always asks questions which come from the "interview schedule," the schedule being a list of fixed choice and open-ended questions which are read to the person being interviewed. Like the questionnaire discussed above, this

interview schedule has been developed and pilot tested
before it is used to collect data. Although some of the
questions may be of the fixed choice variety, there is a
tendency to ask more open-ended questions in the interview. This provides the interviewer (I) with the advantage of being able to ask the respondent (R) probing
questions for clarifying unclear answers. For example:

> I: Have you ever used marijuana?
> R: I used to.
> I: Could you tell me a little more about that?
> R: Well, I used it for about six months.
> I: Are you still using it?
> R: No.
> I: How long ago was that?
> R: I quit about a year ago.

You will notice that these probing questions are not
really new questions but rather questions which bring
out more information or clarify what has been said in
response to the first question.

One of the interesting issues about interviewing is
that individual people respond very differently to being
questioned. Some people give short, brief answers and it is
necessary to draw them
out. Others talk on and
on, sometimes not dis-
cussing the question
you asked; others may
not take the situation
seriously and may even
joke around. The interviewer has to be prepared for
whatever the person does and try to work with that person so that good information is obtained. Usually, interviewers go through a training program in which they
practice handling different types of problems that might
occur during an interview. If you are going to gather

ACTIVITY

At this point you might want to
do Part I of the survey-interview
activity on page 87.

data by interview, you should have some role-playing practice sessions in which you try out the interview schedule on different types of people. Practice will give you experience in handling things that may come up and will give you confidence in the interview situation. If the whole interview team participates in this training, you are better prepared to argue that the situation in which you collected your data was the same in every case.

OBSERVATION

In this section, two methods of observation will be studied, naturalistic observation and participant observation.

NATURALISTIC OBSERVATION

Everybody is an amateur psychologist and sociologist, as we all make inquiries about everyday behavior. One of the things we do frequently is to observe what is going on around us. Naturalistic observation is a method of collecting information which involves observing and recording your observations of naturally occurring events. It is different from participant observation in that the observer is not involved personally as a member of the situation he is observing.

To observe well requires a great deal of concentration. One way to develop this concentration is to observe specific events for short intervals—such as five to ten minutes—and to record as much as you can about what you saw. After several practice sessions you may decide to look only for certain actions, such as the frequency with which people talk to each other at a bus stop or where people sit in a cafeteria

---

ACTIVITY

If there are other people around right now or if it is convenient to find some, spend five minutes watching what they do.

(near the door or in the center of the room). The following questions may be helpful to you in doing research by
naturalistic observation.

*How can I avoid disturbing the process I want to
observe?* One of the things that you do not want to do
is to have your presence affect people so that they somehow change their behavior. Therefore, you need to find
an inconspicuous location from which to observe. If
you were interested in observing behavior at a bus stop,
it would not be helpful to stand ten yards from the stop,
making notes and staring at people. In some circumstances, being watched can cause people to feel extremely self-conscious.

When should I observe people? In a large project
you will probably be observing on several occasions, or
several people may do observations. If you are going to
observe more than once, you should not do all of your
observations at the same time of day unless you are interested only in what happens at that particular time. If
you were going to watch people at a bus stop on several
different occasions, it would *not* be a good idea to do all
observations at 3:00 P.M. because people who go out in
the mid-afternoon might just act differently from people
who catch the bus at 7:30 A.M. to go to work.

What categories of behavior should I select?
Many people who do observational research develop categories for coding people's actions, expressions, or comments. As they watch
people, they count the
frequency with which
people show the behav-
iors in the codes. For
example, at the bus
stop you might count
how often people do such things as talk to someone
else, turn their backs to others, read, etc.

> ### ACTIVITY
>
> At this point you might want to
> do Part I of the observation ac-
> tivity on page 93.

Do I need any equipment? Sometimes you can
film, video tape, or tape record what goes on. (Remem-

ber *Candid Camera?*) However, keep in mind that there are legal limitations and ethical considerations about when you may or may not record what people do or say.

PARTICIPANT OBSERVATION

A participant observer is a person who is both a member and an observer of a social setting. This is very different from naturalistic observation where the researcher has only one role, that of the observer. Most of us know what it means to be a member of a social system, e.g., to be a daughter or son in a family, a student in a class, the head of the hockey team, etc. We have also had experiences as observers. Traveling in a foreign country or even visiting someone else's home provides the experience of observing but not of being a member. Usually people do one thing or the other, doing both at the same time requires practice and timing. Learning to be a participant observer can be a very interesting experience, but it is more difficult than you may imagine when you first hear it described.

Participant observation is a method which is best suited to attempting to understand the relationships between people, the rules of the setting, and what roles different people play in natural settings. For example, a group of psychologists who wanted to better understand the psychology of groups, decided to study a religious group which was predicting that the world would end in two weeks. These psychologists were particularly interested in how the group would act when the world didn't end as they predicted. They decided to have one or two trained observers join the group as members and participate in the group's activities. The group did not know that these members were just "acting" as believers in order to collect data. The participant observers made all their notes in private so that others would not know they were observing, and at the end they wrote a very interesting book which helped us understand the psychology of groups. (There is a valuable methodological appendix in that book [Festinger, et al., see references], which describes some of the important issues in participant observation in a setting where people do not know that you are observing them.)

It is not always necessary for the other members of a setting you are studying to be unaware of your observer role. That decision is made on the basis of whether consciousness of you as an observer would interfere with getting a good understanding of the situation. You may wonder, "Is it ethical not to tell others that I am observing them?" That is a serious question which all researchers must answer. We suggest that your answers to the following questions may help you settle the question in your own mind:

1. Is it necessary not to disclose your observer role to obtain good data?
2. Will either the disclosure of your observing role or the publication of your findings have negative effects for anyone in the setting after you leave it?
3. Do you personally believe that what you are doing is justified and will benefit others?

Now let us turn to the process of becoming a member of a new system so that you can observe it. The first step, which must be planned in advance, is "gaining entry." What is the best way to become a member? If you are studying a factory you may decide to apply for a job; if you are studying parties, you must get invited to one—whatever you do, you want to gain the role of a system member, not someone special. Once you have achieved membership, you need to maintain it.

The most important issue in preparation for participant observation, is taking and writing up field notes. The human brain can only remember so much at a time; therefore, you will need to find times in the setting you are studying when you can make quick notes for yourself. But if people are conscious of your observations and note-taking, you will not be able to observe the system working as it normally does. Since it is unwise to do this in view of others, you will need to create occasions when you can do it. Perhaps every hour or so you may need to go out to your car to get something, go to the bathroom, do an errand, or make a phone call—anything to give you a few quick private moments to jot down in a small notebook what you have observed. Then when you get home, even if you are very tired, you

---

ACTIVITY

After the preparations have been made it is a good idea to practice observing with another person in some setting that isn't the one you are going to use for your research. Try note-taking and then writing up field notes. Compare what you did with what another person in the same setting did. This will give you an idea of what you are missing in your own observations.

---

must sit down and write up in detail what you have observed, using your notes as a guide. It is from this set of field notes that your final report is to be written. Castenada's book *The Teachings of Don Juan,* which is a description of his first-hand experience learning the ways of an Indian medicine man, was prepared from field notes compiled during his experiences.

Obviously you cannot notice and record everything. If you decide on a particular set of categories, your observation will be more focused. You should make a list of the important things to observe in advance and check yourself from time to time to be sure you are attending to all of them.

One of the most interesting recent studies which used participant observation as its method of research was a study of mental hospitals done by David Rosenhan. In this study a group of trained participant observers presented themselves each to a different mental hospital. Each researcher presented himself as mentally ill, described a set of symptoms (everyone described the same symptoms), and requested admission. From that point on they all behaved just the way they would have if they had been outside the walls of the mental hospital. What Rosenhan was interested in was whether, after a person has been labeled "mentally ill," he will be recognized as sane if he acts normal. What he found was that once each of the pseudopatients (the researchers who were participant observers) was hospitalized, all of his behavior was viewed as symptomatic of his illness. In the hospital, only the other patients seemed to recognize that the pseudopatients were sane. Doctors, nurses, and attendants all treated them as mentally ill. In their roles as participant observers, Rosenhan's pseudopatients observed carefully each day the number of contacts patients had with the staff and other specific data which they had agreed in advance to collect. These data are the basis for the interesting observations which Rosenhan makes about institutional life.

THE EXPERIMENT   As previously indicated, the experiment is a controlled situation in which the researcher creates conditions to test specific hypotheses or answer exploratory questions. In its simplest form, the experiment employs two groups: one called an experimental group, to which a treatment of some kind is given; the other called a control group, to which no treatment is given. He (she) then employs the appropriate statistical analysis to determine the effects of his treatment. More complicated experiments involve the systematic variation in treatments administered to several experimental groups.*

There are two types of experiments, laboratory experiments and field experiments. In the former cate-

*There may be some confusion about the term "experimental group." In this context, the phrase "experimental group" refers to a number of subjects who experience the same experimental treatment. This does not necessarily imply that all members of an experimental group participate in the experiment at the same time.

gory, subjects volunteer and are assigned to a special room or laboratory where specific conditions are set up to test hypotheses. For example, subjects might be brought into a special room where the illumination can be systematically varied to test the effects of illumination on reading speed. In the latter category, treatments are administered to subjects in "real life" settings and the reactions of the various experimental groups are compared. For example, the new math might be taught to ten classes of sixth graders and the traditional method of instruction might be taught in ten other classes. After a year, the math ability scores in the two groups of classes could be compared to determine the effectiveness of the new math procedures.

It is beyond the scope of this guide to describe in detail all the steps of scientific experimentation. At the end of this section are several references which will be helpful to students who wish to attempt this form of research. We will outline the more basic principles, particularly as they apply to laboratory research. These might be considered ideals toward which the experimenter should strive. The reader should note that the basic rudiments of designing experiments have already been presented in the design section.

SELECTION AND ASSIGNMENT OF SUBJECTS

The first thing you will need to think about is how to get subjects for your experiment. If you decide to rely upon student volunteers, you could approach various teachers with the offer of a class lecture on your experiment in exchange for the participation of class members. Students may be more than willing to participate in an experiment that will temporarily excuse them from class. An alternative course of action might be to run your experiment after school and have teachers make announcements for student volunteers. All volunteers should be given a general description of what the experiment is about.

Once you obtain the subjects, you will need to figure out a way to assign them to your experimental treatment groups. A recommended procedure is that subjects be randomly assigned to treatment conditions. That is, they should have an equal chance of being placed in any of the experimental treatment groups.

A rough but simple way of doing this might be for you to get a list of subjects who are participating in the experiment. Next to each subject's name you would record a number representing the treatment group to which that subject would be assigned: i.e., "1" if the subject is to be placed in experimental group 1; "2" if the subject is to be placed in experimental group 2, etc. If ten subjects were needed for each group, simply place twenty slips of paper in a hat; ten slips would bear the number "1" and ten would bear the number "2." For each subject, you would draw a slip and place him or her in the group indicated on that slip. When subjects come to the experiment, place them in the experimental condition indicated by their number on the list.

SETTING THE STAGE: DEVELOPING INSTRUCTIONS

It is important that instructions and procedures be standardized as much as possible. Subjects in the same experimental group should all be exposed to identical instructions and procedures. Standardization insures that resulting group differences are due to the researcher's experimental manipulations rather than uncontrolled factors.

The researcher should carefully look over his instructions and procedures to determine whether they are standardized. He should practice reading the instructions until they can be consistently read in the same manner. It is very important that subjects in each experimental session be exposed to instructions that are read in the same tone of voice and with the same facial mannerisms on the part of the experimenter.

Experimenters go to great lengths to standardize

procedures. One common approach is to have the same individual read the instructions to every experimental group. Another approach is to tape record a set of instructions and have these instructions played to all the groups. The latter approach insures absolute consistency but it leaves open the possibility that subjects will perceive the experimental situation as somewhat artificial. For that reason, we would prefer that you try the first approach, and employ one "live," well-practiced experimenter who can administer experimental procedures to all groups.

A related issue concerns the clarity with which instructions are read. The researcher should develop a set of instructions that conveys the essential message of what he expects each experimental group to do. The instructions should be read clearly and concisely, and subjects should be provided with the opportunity to ask questions if the instructions are unclear. The experimenter should answer only those questions that are relevant to the understanding of the instructions. Answers to additional questions should be postponed until the conclusion of the experiment.

Consciously or unconsciously, most subjects try to guess the predictions for their experimental condition. If successful, their performance will be influenced by their knowledge of what is expected of them. To guard against this, the experimenter must endeavor to avoid giving away his predictions. Subjects should be given only the most general information regarding the purpose of the experiment.

To make this point a little clearer, assume that you were conducting an experiment to determine the effects of racial stereotypes on behavior. You might show subjects a scene of an ethnically mixed group of persons sitting in a bus. Subjects would then be asked to reach a consensus on which passenger was responsible for a particular crime. The experimenter could tell the subjects that they are being tested for accuracy in person perception. He would not tell the subjects that he was interested in investigating the effects of racial stereotypes on behavior. The latter statement would undoubtedly influence their responses. Subjects might attempt to demonstrate their "lack of prejudice" by avoiding reference to members of a particular ethnic group in affixing responsibility for the crime.

Studies also indicate that experimenters can unintentionally influence results. Whether consciously or not, experimenters are apt to subtly influence subjects to perform in a manner consistent with the experimental hypotheses. Whenever possible, the person conducting the experimental sessions should be unaware of the predictions for each experimental group. The mechanics of this procedure are quite simple. The researcher finds a friend or colleague who is not intimately acquainted with the research project. The friend or colleague is then trained to run the experiment without being told the hypotheses.

To be effective, your experiment should be credible and have as much impact as possible on the subjects. As you plan your experiment, you might ask yourself: Would the instructions seem credible if I were a subject? Would I find this situation a believable one and get involved in it?

One rule of thumb is to make the manipulation of events as natural and experiential as possible. Thus, if you were interested in how subjects perform under test-taking conditions, you would make the test-taking conditions as natural and involving as possible. You might type up impressive looking test forms. In addition, you might employ a stop watch and tell the subjects that the tests are important measures of intelligence.

DEBRIEFING

Subjects should be debriefed at the conclusion of the experimental session. That is, they should be told something about the purpose of the experiment and the reasons for the manipulations. Interested subjects should be sent results when they become available. In a sense, this information is the subject's reward for participating in the study.

As a condition for debriefing, subjects must promise not to "spoil" future subjects by divulging information about the study. This rarely poses problems. The vast majority of subjects readily agree and keep their word.

PILOT TESTING

Just as with the survey, the researcher should conduct some practice run-throughs of the experiment with persons similar to those who will be subjects in the experiment before the actual experiment is run. Pilot tests are useful in checking the clarity and credibility of experimental procedures and in pinpointing any unforeseen problems that might emerge in conducting the experiment. Typically, the subjects in the pilot tests are asked a number of questions after the experimental session about the procedures: Did they understand the instructions? Did they guess the purpose of the experiment? Did they find the experiment to be credible? etc. If the answers to these questions are less than satisfactory, e.g., most subjects could not understand the instructions, the experimenter should change his experimental procedures before conducting the experiment. Data collected for pilot runs should never be included with the experimental data since a pilot run tests your experimental procedure rather than your hypotheses.

REFERENCES

Castenada, C. *Teachings of Don Juan.* New York: Simon and Schuster, 1973.

Festinger, L., Riecken, H. W., and Schachter, S. *When Prophecy Fails.* Minneapolis: University of Minnesota Press, 1956.

Jahoda, M., Deutsch, M., and Cook, S. W. *Research Methods in Social Relations, Part Two: Selected Techniques.* New York: Dryden Press, 1951.

Lofland, J. *Analyzing Social Settings.* Belmont, Calif.: Wadsworth, 1971. (On observation.)

Orne, M. T. On the social psychology of the psychological experiment: with particular reference to demand characteristics. *American Psychologist,* 1962, 17:776-783.

Rosenhan, D. L. On being sane in insane places. *Science,* 1973, 179:250-258.

COLLECTING DATA

You will want to plan a specific period of time in which to collect all your data. One rule of thumb for all researchers is to try to get organized in advance so that once you start collecting data you can do it as quickly as possible. If you are collecting data in an organization, you need to clear your procedures and arrange the times with the head of that organization. Explaining your project and getting approval often take more time than one might anticipate, so begin that process while you are still preparing for the research.

It is very important—especially if you are collecting data within one social system, e.g., your high school —to do it in a concentrated time period. If some of the people in your sample talk to others who have not taken the questionnaire, interview, or experiment, they may give these untested people ideas about how to respond. Your goal is for everyone to give his own real response and not to be influenced by friends. Therefore, you don't want two people to discuss it with each other before they have both responded.

If it is necessary to have a prolonged period of data collection and you think people may talk with each other and influence each other, here is a suggestion. At the end of each form or in person, ask students not to talk with each other about your research "until X time," e.g., next week, Thanksgiving, etc. Then tell them why: "We want each person to answer for himself, and if other students discuss the questions that can't help but influence what people say." It is also appropriate to tell students how and when they can find out the results of the study in which they participated.

Now that we have discussed the preliminaries, let's consider the details of tabulating data. Suppose you handed out the hypothetical questionnaire shown below. What would you do with the data?

QUESTIONNAIRE

This questionnaire was constructed by class 12-5 for a social science research project. All information will be kept strictly confidential, so please give honest answers. For each question, check the answer that best applies to you.

Sex: male___ female___

1. Do you think marijuana should be legalized for persons over 18 years old?

yes___ no___

2. How often do you use marijuana?

Never   Often
use it |__|__|__|__|__|__|__| use it
        1   2   3   4   5   6   7

3. Have you ever used amphetamines?

___ 1) No, never

___ 2) I tried them once

___ 3) I use them once in a while

___ 4) I use them several times a month

___ 5) I use them several times a week

Let's assume that ten people completed the questionnaire, five males and five females. How would you prepare the data for later statistical analysis? You could keep all the information on ten separate questionnaire sheets, but that would be cumbersome. Most experienced researchers follow the procedure of transferring the information from each subject onto a master coding sheet. In order to do this you must first develop a code so that you can keep track of all the data from each subject. Thus, you might code the males as 100's and the females as 200's. The male questionnaires would be numbered 101 through 105 by placing a number in the upper right hand corner of each questionnaire. The first male questionnaire would be given the number 101, the second 102, etc. Likewise, you might distinguish the females' questionnaires by numbering them from 201 to 205. By using numbers rather than names, you protect the anonymity and confidentiality of each subject. In addition, you will be able to keep track of each questionnaire so that when you transfer the information to a master coding sheet, you do not transfer a given subject's information more than once.

At this point, you would be in a position to transfer the information onto the master coding sheets we have been discussing. To do this, you would take a large sheet of paper and head it with the name of the project and all other identifying information. You would list the code number for each subject and include all the information contained in his or her questionnaire, trying to get as much information as possible onto each coding sheet. A sample coding sheet (Figure 2) is provided on page 47.

Note that the top heading contains the date, the name of the coder, the name of the research team, and other relevant information. This descriptive information is necessary to provide a permanent record of the data. If it were not there, the researcher might look at the data three months later and forget what the coding sheet is about. Underneath the heading is the questionnaire in-

Title of Project: *Survey of Drug Attitudes*   Date: ___3- 15 - 76___

Group: *12-5 Social Studies*   Coder: ___E. P. Hollander___

Subject Number	Question 1		Question 2*	Question 3				
	yes	no	(Scale 1-7)	1	2	3	4	5
Males								
101	/		3	/				
102	/		5		/			
103		/	1	/				
104		/	1	/				
105	/		2	/				
Total	3	2	12	3	/	/	0	0
X̄			2.4					
Females								
201		/	2	/				
202	/		4	/				
203	/		3				/	
204		/	1	/				
205		/	1	/				
Total	2	3	11	4	0	0	/	0
X̄			2.2					

---

*1 = never; 7 = often.

Figure 2: Coding Sheet

formation provided by each subject. Thus, the male whose code number is 101 answered "Yes" to question 1, checked almost the middle of the scale for question 2, and answered 2 ("I tried it once") in response to the third question. The male coded #102 also checked "Yes" to the first question, checked the fifth spot over from the left on the scale (towards the often side) for question 2, and checked 3 ("I take it several times a month") for the third question. The female information follows the same format. Thus, the female coded 201 answered "no" to question 1, checked the second spot over from the left on question 2 (towards the never side) and answered 1 ("no, never") for the third question.

You will note that we have provided totals for the males and females. Thus, three males checked "yes" and two checked "no" for question 1; the males totaled 12 for question 2. For question 3, three males answered "no, never," one answered "once," and one answered "once in a while." For the scale data (question 2) we were also able to calculate averages (means), which are indicated by the notation $\overline{X}$. The mean is simply the total number of scores divided by the number of subjects. If this is confusing to you, don't worry. We will discuss it in more detail when we get to the next section.

What we have presented is a short example of how to prepare coding sheets. However, coding sheets can be developed for more complicated studies involving many more questions.

DANGER! It is very easy to make mistakes when transferring numbers from one sheet to another. That's why in good research laboratories, after one person tabulates the data, another will recheck each entry. Be sure you work out some method to check for errors.

DIVISION OF LABOR

Data collection is one time when it is important to have an organized division of labor within your research team. Here is a list of some of the things that usually have to be done.

1. Check the tasks that your project involves.
2. Add any that are not included in the list.
3. Be sure that one specific person is in charge of each item.

Person Responsible   *Tasks*

_____   a. Preparation of research materials by ____.
                date

_____   b. Permission and arrangements
to collect data from _____
_____ by ____.
     name(s)   date

_____   c. Arrangements for facilities in
which to collect data with
_____ by ____.
     name   date

_____   d. Recruitment and scheduling
of subjects by ____.
             date

_____   e. Selecting and training experimenters by ____.
           date

_____   f. Labeling and filing data as it
is collected by ____.
           date

_____   g. Preparation of method for
tabulating data (e.g., tabulation sheet heading) by ____.
               date

_____   h. Organization of tabulation
(who does what) including
check for errors by ____.
             date

_____   i. Statistical consultation with
math teacher if testing of results is desired.

_____   j. Preparing tables of results for
discussion.

_____   k. Writing up the results.

_____   l. Distributing or publishing the
results.

TESTING YOUR IDEAS

After collecting and organizing your data you may find yourself wondering "so what does it mean?" The numbers you have collected will in fact be the key to understanding the phenomenon you have chosen to study. When doing social science research, we typically study and compare the numerical results obtained from different groups of subjects. Using numbers is a shorthand way of (a) understanding a particular group of people, e.g., the children who watch Sesame Street, and (b) comparing one particular group with another, e.g., the improvement of the Sesame Street group versus the no T.V. control group.

When numbers tell us something about a particular group of subjects, they are called *descriptive statistics*. Thus, we might use descriptive statistics to determine such things as the average reading improvement of students who watch Sesame Street, the average height of students in a high school, or the per game average for members of a particular bowling team. When numbers are used to tell us something about the extent to which two or more groups differ they are called *inferential statistics*. Thus, we might use inferential statistics to determine whether a group of subjects watching Sesame Street improves more than a no T.V. control group, whether students in one high school are taller than students in another high school and finally, whether the Red Rollies have a higher bowling average than the Blue Follies.

DESCRIPTIVE STATISTICS

The word *statistics* often has the connotation of something mysterious and confusing. We would like to give you the tools to make statistics an everyday technique rather than a magician's trick. First, remember that statistics is just shorthand. If you were comparing two groups of 100 persons each, you would not be able to absorb and comprehend the numerical data obtained from each individual. As an alternative, you could take the data from these 200 individuals and summarize it into two groups of data. Group data now becomes a shorthand way of discussing all the individuals within the groups.

Perhaps the most important tools you will use pertain to averaging. Averaging is a method for summarizing large amounts of information. Two kinds of averages are commonly employed: the *mean* and the *mode.* The mean is simply the sum of scores divided by the number of scores. Thus, if you had five members of a bowling team who respectively bowled 110, 125, 175, 134, and 145, the mean or average score for that game would be $(110 + 125 + 175 + 134 + 145) \div 5$ or 689/5 or 133.8. The mode is simply the most common score, the one that occurs the most frequently. It is employed when the researcher is faced with scores that cannot readily be summed and divided to find a mean. Thus, if tests were given and scored from 0 to 100, the researcher could easily find the mean by adding the test scores and dividing by the number of people who took the test. However, if the tests were scored in such a way that five students received A; eight scored B; fifteen C; five D; and two F, the researcher could not sum the scores to find the mean. (It makes no sense to add A's and B's.) However, he could find the mode or most common score. In this case the modal score would be C because more people received C than any other grade.

In addition to finding average scores, researchers are also interested in determining the way in which a particular group of scores are distributed. Two methods for describing a distribution of scores are the *range* and the *frequency distribution.* The range is simply the distance between the highest and lowest scores. To find the range you simply subtract the lowest score from the highest score and add one. Two classes having the same test average might have quite different ranges. Thus, a class having an average score of 50 might have a range of 21 (scores going from 40 to 60, with a range equal to 20 + 1, or 21). Another class having the same average might have a range of 41 (scores going from 30 to 70, with a range equal to 40 + 1, or 41).

The frequency distribution is used to provide the researcher with an overview of the number of instances of each score in a distribution. Frequency distributions can be listed in a table that gives the number of subjects obtaining each score.

As an example consider the following scores of our imaginary Sesame Street group. Each numerical score is the student's improvement in reading ability

---

TABLE 1

Reading Improvement Scores of Students
Watching *Sesame Street*

Score
38
35
33
33
32
32
32
30
30
28
28
27
22
19

Sum of Scores = 420

Number of Scores = 14

---

from September to January. We can get this score by subtracting each student's September reading test score from his or her January reading test score.

The mean for these scores is $420 \div 14 = 30$. The *range* is $(38 - 19) + 1 = 20$. We can obtain a frequency distribution by making a new table that shows (a) all of the possible scores and (b) the number of people who received each score.

This new table will look like the following:

TABLE 2

Frequency Distribution of Reading Improvement
Scores for Students Watching *Sesame Street*

Score (X)	Frequency (f)
40	0
39	0
38	1
37	0
36	0
35	0
34	0
33	2
32	3
31	2
30	2
29	1
28	1
27	0
26	0
25	0
24	0
23	0
22	1
21	0
20	0
19	1
18	0

GRAPHING

Having prepared a table for the frequency distribution, it is now a simple matter to represent the distribution on a graph. One form of graph is the bar graph or
histogram. One simply draws bars to represent the number of cases falling into each interval of scores. Figure 3
illustrates a bar graph set for the data in Table 2. Note
that the vertical line (ordinate) is roughly ¾ as long as

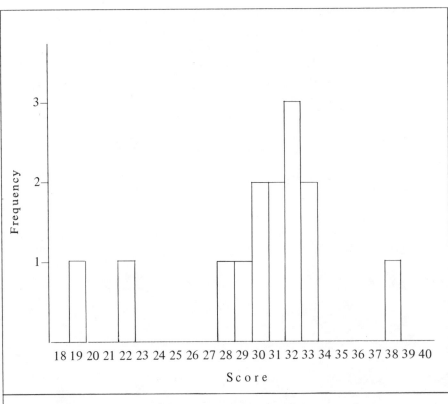

Figure 3:   Histogram of Reading Improvement Scores
for *Sesame Street* Watchers

the horizontal line (abscissa). This is standard procedure
in drawing graphs. Also note that the frequencies on the
ordinate are equally spaced.

Another kind of graph is known as the frequency polygon. This type of graph is drawn by connecting
dots which represent the number of cases falling into
each score. The frequency polygon in Figure 4 shows
the same information as the histogram in Figure 3.

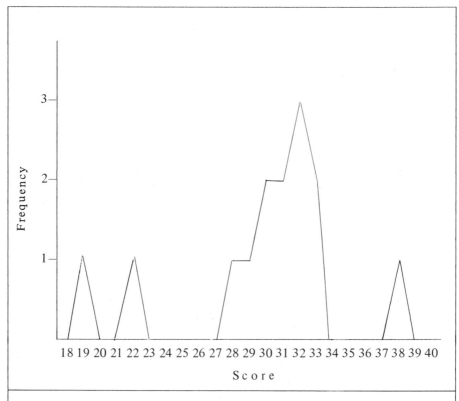

Figure 4:   Distribution Polygon of Reading Improvement
Scores for *Sesame Street* Watchers.

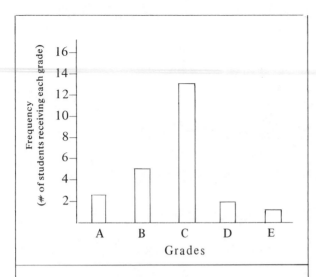

Figure 5: Histogram for Frequency
Distribution of Grades

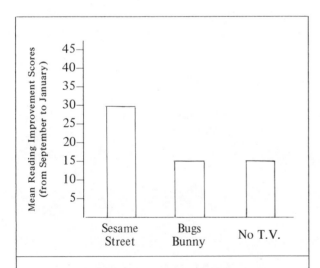

Figure 6: Mean Reading Improvement
Scores for *Sesame Street* Study

The reader should note that graphs can also be used to illustrate category data. The histogram in Figure 5 indicates the number of children receiving scores of A, B, C, D, E on a particular test. Since we are talking about categorical as opposed to numerical data, the bars are separated and not touching. This is a standard convention for dealing with category type data.

You should also note that graphs can be inferentially used to illustrate between-group differences. Figure 6 indicates the (hypothetical) differences in mean reading improvement scores for subjects watching Sesame Street versus those in the Bugs Bunny and no T.V. control groups. It is apparent from the graph that Sesame Street and not T.V. *per se* is responsible for the improvement in reading.

Using numbers to infer group differences is not **INFERENTIAL** always as straightforward as we have made it appear in **STATISTICS** the section on descriptive statistics. In many cases, differences among groups are not as obvious as in the imaginary Sesame Street example we have been using. How can we tell if two or more groups are actually different from each other?

If two classes are given the same test and the mean score for class A is 2 points higher, are we justified in saying that class A is better? Class B might have received a better mean score had the test been given on another day. We can never be certain that a difference between groups, in this case different test grades, is not due to chance. However, statistical tests are available to tell us the possibility or likelihood that group differences are due to chance. Basically, the researcher uses the appropriate statistical test and gets back a number indicating the likelihood that his results are due to chance. Thus, a statistical test might indicate that the apparent group differences between class A and class B have a 50 per cent likelihood of being due to chance. In that case, the researcher would not take the differences seriously. The standard research convention is that the researcher does not take results seriously until there is a five per cent or less likelihood that the results are due to chance. In other words, the researcher has to be at least 95 per cent certain that the results reflect a "real" group difference before he or she takes them seriously. Most statistical tests are quite involved and beyond the scope of this text. If you wish to know more about statistics, we sug-

---

ACTIVITY

Suppose you have three groups taking a test. The members of group A score 50, 62, 57, 71, and 63. The members of group B score 80, 75, 69, 73, and 71. The members of group C score 45, 57, 68, 63, and 69. Find the mean and modal score for each group. Make a graph showing the mean scores for each group.

gest that you confer with a knowledgeable teacher or consult the references provided at the end of this section. While you may not use statistical tests in your research, you should be aware that these tests are an essential part of social science research at the more advanced levels.

HANDLING UNANTICIPATED RESULTS

We may have created the impression that anticipated results are always confirmed. In fact, studies often fail to confirm hypotheses. Unanticipated results reflect one of two things: genuine though unexpected findings or findings that are caused by procedural errors in conducting the study. To guard against procedural errors, the researcher should keep accurate ongoing records of any unusual events occurring over the course of his or her investigation, e.g., a subject failing to answer questions on a survey, a stopwatch malfunctioning. He could then review his records and determine whether unanticipated results were due to procedural errors.

The essential point is that accurate records are indispensable for determining the cause of unanticipated results. A list of possible procedural errors would probably fill up this book. However, in checking his records, the researcher should be aware of the following sources of error: mistakes in calculating data, e.g., numerical errors, mislabeling of data; mechanical errors, e.g., a stopwatch fails in the third experimental session, a tape recorder malfunctions and does not play the instructions when the female subjects are tested; errors of execution, e.g., the experimenter incorrectly reads his instructions or asks survey questions in the wrong order.

If a careful review indicates no procedural errors, the researcher can entertain the possibility that his results are genuine. In that case, he should consider what may be the very exciting implications of his unanticipated results. Particularly when the researcher has worked long and hard on his project, the first reaction to unanticipated results may be disappointment. Sometimes, however, unanticipated results are more interesting than the researcher's original ideas! They can stimulate better research in the future and open up whole new areas of thought and investigation.

REFERENCES

Huff, D. *How to Lie with Statistics.* New York: Norton, 1954.

Runyon, R. P. and Haber, A. *Fundamentals of Behavioral Statistics.* Reading, Mass.: Addison-Wesley, 1972.

Welkowitz, J., Ewen, R. B., and Cohen, J. *Introductory Statistics for the Behavioral Sciences.* New York: Academic Press, 1971.

WRITING UP WHAT YOU HAVE DONE

Science is a public enterprise. That is, we write up what we have done so that other investigators, exploring the same topic, can have access to our results. You may wish to write a report for the school newspaper, a mimeographed description for another class, or perhaps a detailed description for an assembly presentation. For your own purposes, it will suffice to write your report in a clearly organized manner. However, you should be aware that scientific reports are written in a particular form. Those of you who are interested may consult the *Publication Manual of the American Psychological Association,* Washington, D.C.: American Psychological Association, 1967.

PLANNING FURTHER RESEARCH

One study does not answer all the questions you might have posed before conducting the investigation. In fact, some of the information you gather may raise new questions. For this reason, people who have been involved in one research project frequently plan further projects to build upon the results they have previously found. This may not be the case for you, but you should be aware that some scientists spend their entire adult lifetimes investigating a particular problem through a series of co-ordinated studies.

SUMMARY

We have reviewed the basic aspects of social science research. In our short discussion, topics ranging from hypothesis testing, to selecting and training in a particular method, to collecting and analyzing data have been covered. Although you are not yet a sophisticated researcher, you should be in a position to (a) conduct and carry out simple research under a teacher's supervision, (b) understand social science literature, and (c) pursue and understand the more sophisticated references suggested in this manual.

The next section will present descriptive summaries of two quite different social science investigations. This will provide you with a better understanding of the extent and scope of social science research.

part II

research
examples

Two research projects that have been completed and published are included so that you can compare their step-by-step process with the guide you have just read.

EXAMPLE I: AN EXPERIMENT IN UNDERSTANDING DATING

DECIDING WHAT TO INVESTIGATE

While much has been written about romantic love, particularly in our culture, little is really known about how it affects people's behavior. Elaine Walster, a social psychologist at the University of Minnesota, and some of her colleagues were interested in studying romantic love. Although there are many aspects of romantic love that could be investigated in a research project, she decided that it would be useful to know more about how people choose a romantic partner. When a girl looks around for someone to date, how does her own perception of how attractive she is influence which boys she finds romantically interesting and which ones she doesn't find attractive? That was the specific issue that Dr. Walster set out to investigate.

FORMULATING THE HYPOTHESES

Walster thought that people have a "dream girl" or "dream boy" in their imagination who is their ideal image of a romantic partner. She also thought that people have some idea of how attractive they are to others. Since most people are not ideal themselves, they would not expect to find a partner who reaches their ideal. In other words, if you are realistic about who would be interested in dating you, you would make an estimate of how attractive you are and try for a goal that you think is within your social reach.

The researchers had three very specific ideas that they wanted to test. We call these ideas hypotheses because they are predictions about what their research will discover. They were:

1. Individuals who are themselves very socially desirable (physically attractive, personable, possessing great fame or money) will want their romantic partners

to possess more social desirability than those who are less attractive, desirable, or prestigious.

2. If individuals varying in social desirability meet in a social situation, those individuals who are similar in social desirability will most often attempt to date one another.

3. An individual will not only choose a date of approximately his own social desirability, but after actual experience with potential dates of various desirabilities, he will express the most liking for a partner of approximately his own desirability.

These researchers wanted to make specific predictions so they formulated hypotheses. If, however, they were not sure enough to make predictions, they could have developed some exploratory questions such as:

1. Are there differences between people of high and low social desirability in the level of social desirability they expect to find in a romantic partner?

2. Will couples who are similar in social desirability date for a longer period of time than couples who are dissimilar in social desirability?

3. Who would an individual like the most, a romantic partner of higher, equal, or lower attractiveness?

Notice that these exploratory questions do not make predictions. However, they do raise the same questions as the hypotheses above. Hopefully, these questions can be answered in a research project.

SELECTING THE METHOD AND DEVELOPING A DESIGN   There are a number of ways that Walster and her associates could have done their research. They could have *surveyed* large numbers of people and asked them questions about how they selected dates. But there are limitations to a survey. Could people really say how they choose a romantic partner? Some things you might want to know would be of such a personal nature that people might be reluctant to disclose the information needed.

Another approach that could have been used

would have been the experimenters' being in places where people meet socially and *observing* how they interact. One disadvantage of observation is that the behavior you want to study may be very hard to detect by observational techniques. In this case, if you are observing a boy and girl, how can you tell if the boy finds the girl attractive?

Still another approach would be to conduct an *experiment* in which the researchers change a situation or control some aspect of it to see what effect that change has on the way people behave. For example, the researchers could use a girl who thinks of herself as very attractive or not very attractive in their experiment. They could arrange three situations where she meets a different type of boy in each: a friendly, highly desirable boy; a friendly, moderately desirable boy; and a boy who is friendly but not very socially desirable. They would then look to see which type of boy she would most like to have as a partner. Please note: this would be called an experiment because the researchers would be controlling the types of boys the subject would be meeting.

Elaine Walster decided that an experiment would be the best way to test her ideas to see if they were true. You can imagine, though, that if she had asked people to come into a laboratory in a university to be tested, they would probably be very self-conscious. If they were too self-conscious, they might not have acted the same way they would if they were in their normal situation. Since she wanted to know whether her ideas were true in normal life, Walster cleverly designed an experiment that could be run in a setting where people went to meet each other. We call these "field experiments." In this case the experiment was run at a freshman dance at a large university where partners were matched by computer.

You will remember that each of Walster's hypotheses involved the social desirability of individuals as dates. Since social desirability is a complex concept, she needed something clear and observable for measuring the social desirability of subjects in her experiment. Walster selected physical attractiveness as the "indicator" of social desirability. That is, she picked one aspect (physical attractiveness) which she thought was a good representative of the concept. In this case physical attractiveness was chosen as an "indicator" for social desirability.

How did Elaine Walster design the experiment? If you examine the hypotheses carefully, you'll see that to come to any conclusions she will need to make some comparisons. Specifically, she will need to compare couples who are of equal attractiveness and couples where one is more attractive than the other. That means she must either find or create a situation in which there are quite a few couples who are equal or unequal in physical attractiveness. In this case she decided to create the situation. Here's how she went about it.

The dance was advertised along with 87 other events in a handbook received by all incoming freshmen. In fact, however, the dance was not a regular Welcome Week event and had been set up solely to test the hypotheses. The handbook advertisement describing a Computer Dance said: "Here's your chance to meet someone who has the same expressed interests as yourself." Freshmen were told that if they would give the computer some information about their interests and personalities, the computer would match them with a date. Tickets were $1.00 per person; both men and women purchased their own tickets. Long lines of subjects appeared to buy tickets on the opening day; only the first 376 male and 376 female students who appeared were accepted.

For experimental purposes, the ticket sale was set up in an extremely bureaucratic style. The student walked along a table in the foyer of the Student Union. First, a student sold him a ticket. He moved down the table, and a second student checked his identification card to make sure he was a student and told him to report to a large room two flights above. When the subject arrived at the upstairs room, a third student met him at the door, handed him a questionnaire with his student code number stamped on it, and asked him to complete the questionnaire at an adjoining table. A fourth student directed him to a seat. (Proctors around the room answered the subject's questions and discouraged talking.)

The four bureaucrats were actually college sophomores who had been hired to rate the physical attractiveness of the 752 freshmen who purchased tickets to the dance.

As each student passed, the four raters rapidly and individually evaluated the subject's physical attractiveness on an eight-point scale, going from 1 ("Extremely unattractive") to 8 ("Extremely attractive"). Obviously, these attractiveness ratings had to be made very quickly; usually the rater had less than one or two seconds to look at the subject before making his evaluation, and rarely did the rater get to hear the subject say more than "O.K." or "Thank you." The briefness of this contact was by design. Since one aspect of social desirability had been chosen as an index of total desirability, Walster wanted to be sure, as far as possible, that the raters were assessing only that aspect. She did not want ratings of attractiveness to be heavily influenced by the subject's personableness, intelligence, voice quality, etc.

TRAINING IN THE METHOD

In most writeups of research, the training is not described. Here are some examples of training which Walster may have done to improve the experiment before she ran it:

1. Before the four sophomores actually did a quick rating of the subjects' attractiveness in the experiment, they may have practiced this procedure. That way they could agree in advance on the way they would make the judgments.

2. The questionnaire may have been tried out ("piloted") on students not in the experiment before it

was used, to be sure that all the questions were clear and that everyone understood them the same way.

3. Experimenters at the dance may have practiced what they were to say in administering the second questionnaire so each would say the same thing.

COLLECTING DATA

The students filled out questionnaires. These provided information about how attractive and popular the subject thought he or she was, what the date was expected to be like, and how good the subject felt about himself (self-esteem). Before the dance, individuals were randomly matched with each other. This provided a good cross-section of people who were matched with someone of a (1) higher, (2) lower, and (3) equal level of attractiveness. During the intermission of the dance the students' impressions of their dates were assessed. Six months after the dance each person was contacted to determine how often they had dated the partner with whom they had been matched.

DRAWING CONCLUSIONS

The first hypothesis was tested in two ways. First, by comparing how attractive a subject was with how attractive he expected his date to be. A comparison was also made between how attractive a subject was and how critically he rated his date during intermission. If people who are highly attractive require that their partners be highly attractive also, then the researchers could expect highly attractive individuals to be significantly more critical of their dates than would subjects of lesser attractiveness. From the data they collected, the researchers were able to confirm their first hypothesis: the attractive students consistently judged their dates more harshly than did the less attractive students.

To test the second hypothesis, a comparison was made to determine if couples who were alike in social attractiveness were likely to continue dating. That turned out not to be the case in this study. People who were equally matched in attractiveness were not any more likely to continue dating than those who were unevenly matched.

The researchers assumed from the third hypothesis that subjects would over-rate partners who were on their own level of attractiveness. The test for this hypothesis, then, would be to determine if this actually happened. But subjects did not over-rate partners when their partners were of approximately their own level of desirability. So the third hypothesis was not supported either.

You will notice that not every idea of the researcher was confirmed. This is often true in research. However, the fact that the first hypothesis was confirmed gives them a good start in thinking about future research. They appear to be on the right track since they have found that more attractive persons judged their dates more harshly. What they still don't understand (since the second and third hypotheses were not confirmed) is how that affects the continuance of a dating relationship. They suggest that, while attractiveness may be very important on first meeting, other factors may become more important as the relationship progresses.

WRITING UP WHAT YOU HAVE DONE

The study we have been describing has been written up and published in the *Journal of Personality and Social Psychology*. When you write up the results of your project you might consider the local newspaper, your school paper, or a mimeographed write-up to be handed out to other students and interested persons.

PLANNING FURTHER RESEARCH

Just how important is physical attractiveness? The study described here indicates that early in a relationship it is important for 18-year-old college students. Perhaps this would not be true for people of a different age group. Or, as we have suggested already, even if it is important on first meeting, other factors such as intelligence, likes-dislikes, being an insecure college freshman, or something else become more important. Questions

like these would be the basis for further research. No social scientist expects a single study to answer all the
questions, but each study helps to clarify psychological
processes and shapes our thinking about the next piece
of research.

REFERENCES   Berscheid, E. and Walster, E. H. *Interpersonal Attrac-
tion.* Reading, Mass.: Addison-Wesley, 1969, pp. 105-
114.
Walster, E., Aronson, V., Abrahams, D., and Rottmann,
L. Importance of physical attractiveness in dating behavior. *Journal of Personality and Social Psychology,*
1966, 5:508-516.

EXAMPLE II: A SURVEY OF STUDENT POWER IN INNOVATIVE HIGH SCHOOLS

**DECIDING
WHAT TO
INVESTIGATE**
      Joan Chesler and her colleagues Glorianna Wittes
and Dale Crowfoot were part of a group in the School of
Education at the University of Michigan called the Education Change Team. The team was active in the early
70's studying student unrest and protests in high schools
around the country. Together they collected data linking unrest in high schools to students' beliefs that there
was racism and student oppression in their school.

      Chesler and her colleagues took the results of
that research as a jumping off place for a separate research project. They decided to study high schools that
were not organized in a traditional way, but were trying
out new governance structures, new patterns of decision
making. "Governance structure" refers to the opportunities available to people in an organization to have influence over the organization. For example, in traditional
high schools the principal and administrators have the
most power over decisions, department heads and teachers are next in power, and students are last. Even if there

is a student government, it is often either advisory, i.e., it has no real power, or is not well connected with the real centers where decisions are made. In some innovative schools, however, the whole school may meet to make decisions, while in others a council made up of students, teachers, and sometimes parents make all decisions, including who shall be the principal administrator, what courses shall be taught, and who shall be hired or fired. In one school of this type the council was composed of ten students, five faculty, and five parents.

Previous research indicated that in traditionally structured high schools, minority groups of all kinds have a difficult time getting heard or having influence in decisions. Chesler's group decided to find and study a small group of innovative high schools having different types of governance. They hoped that from this study some general principles would emerge which would be applicable for schools that wanted a governance structure in which both minority groups and the majority within the school could have some influence over school policy.

EXPLORATORY QUESTIONS

The basic exploratory question that this study proposed to investigate was whether student power and participation in the governance and curriculum of a school offer definite benefits to all members of the school community. Specifically they expected that:

a. In the innovative high school, students and other oppressed groups would be able to make school policies and programs directly responsive to what they needed.

b. Relationships between students, teachers, and administrators would be more mutual, less unilateral (i.e., a two-way street, not just one-way with the adults managing the students).

c. All members of the school would be able to deal with differences, confront and find productive solutions to conflict, and gain self-assertive styles of thought and action.

SELECTING A   These researchers decided that if they really want-
METHOD   ed to find new models for schools, they would need to
locate and intensively study a number of individual
schools. What would be the best way to study the governance structure of a high school and its effects on students, teachers, and administrators? That was the question they had to answer as they decided on a method.
Since they wanted to study a whole social system, obviously the idea of doing an experiment was not practical.
They would have had to set up a whole experimental
high school and run it!

DESIGN AND
TRAINING IN THE
METHODOLOGY   Because it was a big project, they decided to use
more than one method. The most important data was
obtained from interviews with students, teachers, and
administrators at the high school and from a survey-
questionnaire that was administered to school partici-
pants. Some additional data was collected by observation of classes and halls, by reading local and school
newspapers, and by reading reports of meetings at the
school.

With an interview survey, it was possible for the
researchers to ask in-depth questions that would tap
people's attitudes and feelings about the high school as a
means of exploring the questions they had raised.

Now we will turn in more detail to the specific
issues in design and method that these researchers en-
countered:

1. How did they select the high schools they
studied?
2. How did they decide who to interview in the
high school?
3. Who collected the data and how were they
trained?

SELECTION OF HIGH SCHOOLS

The research team decided to study six high schools very carefully. They decided that the six high schools selected should:

1. represent different types of innovation;
2. be different in size;
3. be located in different sections of the country;
4. be both public and private;
5. include white and inter-racial student bodies;
6. have an innovative decision-making structure that had been in operation long enough to be able to judge its performance;
7. be willing to be studied by the research team.

They succeeded in locating six very interesting schools that met their criteria. If you are interested in reading in more detail about these schools, references to the original sources are given at the end of the example.

DECIDING WHOM TO INTERVIEW

The next decision Chesler and her colleagues had to make was who should be interviewed in order to get a complete picture of the effects of the schools' decision-making structures. Before reading any further we suggest that you stop a minute and consider the following question: "If I were part of a team of researchers coming to. my high school who would I want to interview to get a complete picture of the school?" You may want to jot down some of your ideas before reading further.

In this case two types of samples were selected and interviewed. (A "sample" is just what it sounds like, a small percentage of a larger group.) One sample was selected because of its role in the school. This makes a lot of sense when you consider that the researchers were studying decision-making. They wanted to interview the key administrators and the key officers in student organizations because these people were important in decisions that were made. The other sample was a random sample of students and teachers. In selecting this group, the researchers made sure that the proportion of males and females and of ethnic groups at the school was similar to its representation. For students, they made sure that they included students in all grades and programs, and students with differing degrees of involvement in high school activities. For teachers, they included some teachers from all departments, teachers with differing years of experience and with a variety of educational philosophies. In this study, two random samples were used. One was interviewed and answered a brief questionnaire, the other filled out a longer written questionnaire. By using an "important-role" sample and random samples the authors believed that they could get data that would help them answer their exploratory questions.

THE INTERVIEW-SURVEY TEAM

Prior to collecting the data, a team of five or six researchers was organized and trained for each of the schools. You will recall in our description of data collection we emphasized the importance of collecting the data rapidly. The leader of each team visited the school in advance and identified who should be interviewed. Then the research team came in for a week, collected their data, and left.

Chesler, Wittes, and Crowfoot gave careful thought to the issue of who should do the interviewing. They decided that they would get the most accurate information if the interviewers were similar to those they were to interview. For that reason, each team was composed of high school students (from another school) and adults. For the same reason, the research teams were composed to reflect the racial balance of the high school. For example, in one high school that was about 50% white, 35% black and 15% Oriental, the research team was composed of students and adults of whom 3 were white, 2 were black, and 1 was Oriental. This permitted adults to interview the administrators and teachers, students to interview students, blacks to interview blacks, etc.

PRE-TRAINING
        Before going to their high school, each team had a period of training. Within the team they practiced the interview by role playing. One team member was the interviewer and another would role play a member of the high school. This practice helped them standardize the interview and anticipate different problems that might arise in the interview situation. As a second step they got permission to go into a nearby high school (*not* the one selected for the study) and conduct interviews. This gave the team an opportunity to pilot test the interview questions and the printed survey questionnaires that they planned to administer.
        The interview itself was organized to answer the exploratory questions. Each interview was tape recorded. Here are two examples from the interview "schedule" of the types of questions that were asked of the "important-role" sample and of a random sample:

About the general atmosphere of the school:
        Question: Pretend you are making a film of this
                    school. What would you include in this
                    film to demonstrate its essential flavor
                    to the viewer?
        Probes (to be used by interviewer if needed): probe
                    for intergroup relations, morale, commit-
                    ment, satisfaction-dissatisfaction.

About the governance of the school:
        Questions: Is there a formal governing organization?
                    Who belongs to it?
                    How is membership obtained?
                    How often does it meet?
                    What sort of decision areas does it de-
                        termine?

How much power do different role
groups have?
Do you belong?
How much energy does it take?
What are the rewards and punishments
for participating in this body?

At the end of each interview the person being interviewed was asked to complete a brief printed questionnaire which collected additional data bout control and
influence in that school. Here is an example of one of
those questions:

How much influence do you think each of the following groups
has in deciding what *changes* are made in the programs and courses
offered at your school?

This is how it is *now*

Teachers	none () () () () () great deal
Superintendent's Office	() () () () ()
Students	() () () () ()
Principal and assistants	() () () () ()
Guidance counselors	() () () () ()
Parents of students	() () () () ()
You, yourself	() () () () ()

This is how I'd *like* it to be

Teachers	none () () () () () great deal
Superintendent's Office	() () () () ()
Students	() () () () ()
Principal and assistants	() () () () ()
Guidance counselors	() () () () ()
Parents of students	() () () () ()
You, yourself	(.) () () () ()

In order to reach a broader segment of the school
a more comprehensive survey questionnaire was administered to a second random sample of students and teachers. In the smaller schools it was administered to every-

one; in the larger schools to a random sample. An example of one of the questions from that instrument:

- How many students at this school are friendly and easy to approach?   none ( ) ( ) ( ) ( ) ( ) almost all

- How many students here seem excited about their work and really seem to enjoy learning?   none ( ) ( ) ( ) ( ) ( ) almost all

- How many teachers at this school are friendly and easy to approach?   none ( ) ( ) ( ) ( ) ( ) almost all

- How many teachers here seem excited about their work and really seem to enjoy teaching?   none ( ) ( ) ( ) ( ) ( ) almost all

TABULATING AND SUMMARIZING THE DATA

The data were summarized in two ways. Because each high school had some interesting and unique characteristics in its particular model for innovative decision making, each school was separately studied in depth as a first step. Complete findings about each individual school are reported in the references at the end of this example.

The second step, and the one of interest to us because it answers the exploratory questions, was to look at the data from all six schools. You may be wondering how the researchers could make any sense out of such a complex amount of data. Of course, the questions they wanted to answer guided the data collection. After it was collected, it had to be summarized and tabulated in several different ways.

CODING

When open-ended questions are asked, the responses must be coded into specific categories so that they can be organized and compared. A number of themes were developed by the research teams as categories for examining the data. Interviews from all six

schools were then examined for similarities and differences around each theme or category. The major results
of the study are drawn from the conclusions reached by
comparing schools across each category.

The major categories used in coding were:
1. The history of the innovation
2. The process of introducing the innovation
3. The effects of size of high school on the innovation
4. Relations between groups in the high school, e.g.,
   teachers/students, blacks/whites
5. Student power
6. Individual autonomy vs. community interests
7. Evidence of pluralism (smaller interest group
   needs met)
8. Atmosphere of the school

TABULATING

In addition to coding, of course, the data from
the written questionnaires had to be tabulated and summarized in much the same way as we have demonstrated
in our description of that process earlier.

**CONCLUSIONS
OF THE STUDY:**
**Results of the
Exploratory
Questions**
The first important difference these researchers
found was a difference between student autonomy and
student power. "*Autonomy* is the individual student's
freedom to choose his courses and select his teachers;
i.e., his freedom to determine issues that affect him personally. *Power* is the students' collective ability to influence not only curriculum decisions, but also school policy and management issues" (Chesler, pp. 270-271). In
all of these innovative schools students had considerable
autonomy or control over their own education, but in
only a few did they also have power or influence over institutional decisions that affected their lives. In fact, students in some schools were confused about the difference
between the two kinds of influence. They thought that
since they had a lot of personal freedom of choice (au-

tonomy), they had power. Chesler points out that only in schools where students had both autonomy and power did they have real influence over the decisions that affected their lives at school.

Several of the schools that expected that a lot of autonomy for students would generate active participation in all phases of school decision making found that this did not occur. Further, it was found that in schools that were most successful at sharing decision-making power: (1) formal governance processes were clear, known to all; (2) informal communication processes between adults and youth were open and trusting; (3) students were organized in subgroups representing their differing interests; (4) information was readily available to all members of the school; (5) formal power was part of the curricular process, not an "extra"; and (6) some training in how to organize and use political power was available to students to counteract the early training received by young people in being dependent on adult authority.

A second variation they found was the difference between the types of power over school affairs that students were able to exercise. In some schools students had *formal* power; that is, they had voting rights on various school committees and councils where important decisions about the school were made. In other schools students had *informal* influence; there was much informal communication and discussion among students, administrators, and teachers. What these researchers found was that unless students had both kinds of power, both informal communication and formal representation, they were not apt to have much power in their school.

A third issue which emerged in examining the data was the contrast between individual freedom (autonomy) and social justice. Since a main interest of Chesler and her colleagues was school organization in which minority groups within the high school have some influence, they wanted to look very carefully at their data for what they call "cultural pluralism." In other words,

are smaller groups of students who are not in the majority in a school also able to influence decision making in
such a way that they get some things that they want?
One thing the researchers found was that in schools with
a big emphasis on individuals doing their own thing (autonomy), it was difficult for groups of students with
similar interests to get together and organize. Apparent-
ly, when student interests were diverted into individual
activity, little time and few opportunities were available
for the pursuit of common needs. For the most part,
real pluralism was absent from these innovative schools.
This discovery caused the authors to question whether
individual growth as a major school goal did not slow
down the development of social justice (real pluralism)
in high schools.

It appears that the exploratory questions provided a useful framework for examining the differences between schools and clarifying the original expectation of
the researchers, as well as for generating some new ideas
that could be tested out as hypotheses in future research.

A final note about this research is in order. Unlike the experimental example presented earlier, this research did not have very precise hypotheses that were
tested. This does not mean that in interview-survey studies there cannot be tight hypotheses—obviously there
can be. In this case, the researchers were just beginning
their exploration. You may have wondered where the
control group was in this study. (There wasn't any.) That
would be an important element in any further research.
No piece of research is absolutely perfect, and this one
has its flaws. We have chosen to present it because the
subject matter is interesting and because it may give you
an idea of what research that tries to answer exploratory
questions is like.

In this study the researchers used several methods—interview, survey, observation, and the examination
of documents—to try to understand decision-making

processes in carefully selected innovative high schools. As a result of their research, they were able to make a number of distinctions about student power, which led them to formulate some ideas about what conditions lead to students' having real power and control, not only over their own school life, but also over the environment in which they work and learn.

REFERENCES

Chesler, J. Innovative governance structures in secondary schools. *The Journal of Applied Behavioral Science,* 1973, 9:261-280.

Wittes, G., Chesler, J., and Crowfoot, D. *Student Power: Practice and Promise.* New York: Citation Press, in press.

part III

activities

Part III provides the student with the opportunity to participate actively in research exercises. Eight activities are included. The first three activities offer the opportunity to conduct a survey, observation study, and experiment from start to finish. These activities are fully explained and each should take roughly a period of class time to complete. We have provided a complete set of instructions including the hypotheses to be tested, the required materials, a description of the data analysis, and suggestions for further studies that build upon these activities.

The latter five activities place the burden of creativity squarely on the shoulders of the student. These exercises provide students with the opportunity to develop their own hypotheses, formulate their own research designs, and decide upon the best method for testing their hypotheses. They serve as a direct prelude for the student (or class) who wishes to design and carry out his own study. These exercises should each take roughly a class period to conduct. We suggest that it is preferable but not essential that the class participate in the first three exercises before proceeding to the latter activities.

SURVEY ACTIVITY

This exercise is divided into two parts. The first part is designed to provide you with experience in interviewing and conducting a survey. We have especially constructed this exercise to familiarize you with the types of problems faced by interviewers. The second part is designed to provide you with experience in analyzing survey data. You will have the option of either making up your own survey or using one we have prepared for you.

PART 1: INTERVIEWING & ADMINISTERING A SURVEY

Interviewing is a skill that requires practice, patience, and the skill to keep subjects from straying off the topic. In this exercise you will form groups of three to practice interviewing one another with the sample survey that follows. The information obtained from the interview will be used in the next exercise on analyzing surveys. Within each group of three, rotate roles, with one of you being the interviewer, the second the interviewee (the person who is interviewed), and the third an observer. The interviewer conducts the interview by asking the questions in the survey and recording the answers. The observer watches while the survey is being administered and makes notes pertaining to what the interviewer does well and what the interviewer might improve (a guide for the observer is printed below). At the end of the interview, the observer should share his observations, and all three persons should discuss the interview and then rotate positions; the interviewer becomes the interviewee; the interviewee, the observer; and the observer, the interviewer. By the end of the exercise, you should all have experience in each of the three positions.

SAMPLE SURVEY
Attitudes Toward High School Testing Policy

Hello, I'm_____ from high school class_____.
We're investigating student attitudes toward HS testing policy. I'd
like to ask you a few questions to sample your opinions.

                    male___   female___   (interviewer fill in)

1. What type of test do you prefer to take?

              essay___   true-false___   multiple choice___

2. Would you prefer a "Pass-Fail" grading system to the present
   system of grading?

                              yes___   no___

3. How anxious do you generally get while taking tests? (Interviewer shows interviewee question and has him check the appropriate space on the line.)

   |_____|_____|_____|_____|_____|
         5   4   3   2   1
       very   not at all
      anxious   moderately   anxious

4. What is your present grade average?_____

5. If tests were given on the honors system with no teacher present, how likely is it that you would cheat?

   |_____|_____|_____|_____|_____|
         1   2   3   4   5
     extremely   extremely
      unlikely   likely

6. What are your specific post-high school plans?
   _____
   _____

7. How much responsibility should students have for making up
   test questions?
   _____
   _____

Guide for Observers

    Be particularly alert to the following points:

1. Does the interviewer read the questions clearly?
2. Does the interviewer read the questions in an unbiased manner?
3. Does the interviewee seem to understand the questions?

**VARIATION
ON PART 1**

    When conducting survey interviews, you will probably find that some persons are easier to interview than others. The class may want to think about people they know and anticipate some of the kinds of problems one could have on an interview. Three different types of people who come to mind are "The Talkative Topic Jumper," who wants to talk a lot and continually wanders from the topic; "The Shy Whisperer," who has to be continually prompted to say anything; and "The Overpersonal Extrovert," who is very friendly and seeks to talk about you and other personal subjects unrelated to the survey. As you take turns administering the survey, you may wish to have each person who plays the interviewee act as The Talkative Topic Jumper, The Shy Whisperer, The Overpersonal Extrovert, or other types thought up by the class. Each prospective interviewee should play a different one of these roles when his turn comes.

    Remember, the goal of the interviewer is to control the interview and obtain answers to as many survey questions as possible. If the interviewee does not fully answer the questions, prompt him to give more complete answers, e.g., "Could you tell me more?", "Is there anything more you wish to add?" If the interviewee tries to change topics, politely remind him of the task at hand, e.g., "We can talk about that later, after the survey."

**PART 2: ANALYZING
A SURVEY**

    You have two options in this exercise. The first alternative is that you analyze the survey data from Part I.

Alternative 2 is that the class makes up, administers, and analyzes its own survey. This survey can be conducted within the class, or it can involve interviewing or administering questionnaires to students in other classes or people in the community. Or you could do both; you could administer and analyze the sample survey and then make up and carry out one on your own.

If you are going to analyze the sample survey, read through the sections on collecting and analyzing data before proceeding. You will also need to figure out some way to divide the labor. Sample coding forms (Figures 7 and 8) are provided on pages 96 and 97 to help you analyze the data when you tabulate it.

After tabulating the sample survey, here are some things you might do:

1. Check the percentage of students checking "yes" and "no" to the various questions.
2. Look at differences between males and females and between college bound and non-college bound students in test-taking preferences.
3. Investigate whether students who have different test-taking preferences react differently to tests. For example, are students who prefer a pass/fail grading system more anxious when taking tests than students who prefer a more traditional system? You can check this by comparing the mean test anxiety scores on question 3 for students who check "yes" and students who check "no" on the pass/fail question.
4. See if students who check the high end of the anxiety scale (4 or 5) are more likely to cheat than those who check the moderate or low end (1, 2, or 3).
5. There are about twenty other analyses you can do, depending upon your interest and ingenuity.
6. You may also wish to make up graphs to illustrate your results.

Sample Coding Form—Survey Example

Date _____   Coder _____   Sample Class _____

Subject Number	Question 1 Essay	T-F	M.C.	Question 2 yes	no	Question 3 Anxiety Scale (1-5)	Question 4 put in average	Question 5 Cheating Scale (1-5)
Males								
101								
102								
103								
etc.								
Females								
201								
202								
203								
etc.								

Figure 7: Survey Attitudes Toward High School Testing
Part A: Objective Questions

Sample Coding Form—Survey Example

Date_____   Coder_____   Sample Class____

Subject Number	Question 6 A	B	C	D	E	F	Question 7 A	B	C	D
Males										
101										
102										
103										
etc.										
Females										
201										
202										
203										
etc.										

o   o   o   o   o   o   o   o   o   o   o   o   o   o   o   o   o   o   o   o   o   o   o   o   o   o   o

Technical Notes: Content Coding Categories

The following codes have been developed for open-ended questions 6 and 7. For these questions, code the subject's answers into the most appropriate category. If more than one category seems appropriate (e.g., a subject indicates that he plans to go into the armed forces and later attend college), code the subject's answer for more than one category.

Content Coding Question 6

a. college or technical training
b. armed forces
c. marriage, no work
d. seek work
e. travel, beach or ski bum
f. other

Content Coding Question 7

a. students have total responsibility
b. teachers have total responsibility
c. shared responsibility of student and teacher
d. other

Figure 8:   Survey Attitudes Toward High School Testing
Part B: Content Coding

OBSERVATIONAL ACTIVITY

The following activity will give you experience in observational methods. We have divided the activity into two parts. Part 1 is designed to sharpen your powers of observation. You will find that if you spend five or ten minutes observing events in a particular social setting, you will be aware of many things which had previously escaped your attention. Part 2 is somewhat more involved. You will be using observational methods to test specific hypotheses. Parts 1 and 2 should be undertaken on separate class days.

PART 1: GENERAL OBSERVATIONS

Each student is to spend 10 minutes observing activities that occur in the cafeteria. If possible, you should use your observations to develop hypotheses or exploratory questions pertaining to lunchroom activity. When everyone returns to class after completing the assignment, you can break up into small groups of four or five students to discuss what you learned from your observations. After five or ten minutes of discussion, the groups can share (a) what they learned about lunchroom activities and (b) the hypotheses or exploratory questions that they have developed.

PART 2: USING OBSERVATIONAL METHODS TO TEST A PARTICULAR HYPOTHESIS

Some researchers who have investigated psychological differences between the sexes have proposed that males tend to be more "thing" oriented while females are more "person" oriented. In the social setting of the lunchroom, this would lead to the following hypotheses: (1) Males spend a greater percentage of their time looking at their utensils because of their "thing" orientation. (2) Likewise, females spend a greater percentage of their time looking at other people because of their "person" orientation.

PROCEDURE   A.   *Selection of Subjects for Observation*

You will each observe four persons (two males and two females) as they begin to eat their lunch. Spend five minutes observing each individual. In order to test the hypotheses, we shall need to have comparable observation procedures followed by each student observer, i.e., all observers must follow the same procedure. Hence, you should follow these rules when selecting your subjects for observation.

1. Select your subjects in the following order: subject 1, male; subject 2, female; subject 3, female; subject 4, male.
2. Remember to select subjects who are starting to eat their lunch. Do not select subjects who are almost finished eating.
3. Select people who are eating in a group.
4. Select people who are sitting at another table. This way they will be less likely to notice you and be influenced by your observations.
5. Observe people you do not know. A stranger will be less likely to notice you and be influenced by your observations.
6. Select subjects who have some drinking utensil with them: glass, milk container, etc.

B.   *Collection of Data*

Basically, you will be observing and noting down what each subject does while holding his drinking utensil. To simplify the procedure, make up a chart similar to the sample chart (Figure 9) on page 100 and use it to record your observations. Every time the subject picks up a drinking utensil, note whether he or she has spent the majority of the time (while the glass or utensil was in his or her hand) looking at the utensil or looking at people in the lunchroom. When the subject puts down the glass or carton, make a slash in the appropriate box in your chart. Repeat this procedure each time the subject lifts up the drinking utensil during the five-minute observation period.

	Number of times picked up utensil and looked at it	Number of times picked up utensil and looked at others	Percentage of times looked at utensils
Practice Subject	*III*= 3	*THH* =5	5/8 = 62.5%
Subject #1 Male			
Subject #2 Female			
Subject #3 Female			
Subject #4 Male			

Figure 9:   Sample Chart for Observations.

[Note: Before you begin the actual observations, spend a few minutes observing a practice subject. This will help you to familiarize yourself with the observation and scoring procedures.]

C.   *Calculating Results*
      When you have finished your observations, you should have three results for each person: (1) the number of times the person looked at others, (2) the number of times the person looked at the utensil, and (3) the *percentage* of times the person looked at the utensil. The percentage of times is calculated as follows:

% of times looked at utensil =

$$= \frac{(\# \text{ times looked at utensil}) \times 100}{(\# \text{ times looked at utensil}) + (\# \text{ times looked at others})}.$$

D. *Class Presentation of Data*

After the assignment is completed, the results of the class observations can be calculated. To do this, the students should pass all of their data sheets to one person. The teacher or a designated assistant can record the "percentage of times looked at utensil" results for males and females in separate columns on the blackboard. Students can then calculate the average (mean) percentage of times that males and females looked at utensils. For clarity, see the sample results shown below in Table 3.

TABLE 3

Sample Results

% times males looked at utensils		*% times females looked at utensils*	
Subject #1	100%	Subject #1	50%
2	50%	2	50%
3	75%	3	25%
4	33%	4	25%
5	42%	5	30%
	300% ÷ 5		180% ÷ 5
	$\overline{X} = 60\%$		$\overline{X} = 36\%$

In these sample results the mean percentage of times that men look at their utensils is 60%. The mean percentage of times that females look at their utensils is 36%. One can see that males spend a greater percentage of their time looking at their utensils than females do. It follows that females spend a greater percentage of their time looking at others than males do.

E. *Discussion*

If the hypotheses are confirmed, males should spend a greater percentage of their time looking at their utensils than should females. Conversely, females should spend a greater percentage of their time looking at people. You might discuss whether the results seem to confirm the hypotheses. You might also discuss the experiences and problems you had conducting your observations. Finally, you might wish to plan future studies of cafeteria behavior. For example, you might wish to investigate whether males eat differently when in the company of males as compared with their eating habits in the company of females.

EXPERIMENT

We have designed a brief experiment that you can conduct. This will provide you with first-hand experience in the methods of experimentation. Read the material below before you begin the experiment.

NOTE TO STUDENTS

This experiment is designed to show how various mnemonic or memory devices can increase learning. You will serve as subjects, your teacher as experimenter. For this experiment to work, you must be totally naive while participating. Therefore, we ask that *you not turn ahead and read the instructions for the experiment.* After it's over, you will have ample opportunity to do so. Remember, your performance won't affect your grade. Hence, there is no reason to "cheat" by peeking ahead at the instructions. Listen to your teacher and turn only to the pages he asks you to read.

NOTE TO TEACHER

You will serve as the experimenter for the following experiment. Please turn to the next page, where you will find a complete set of instructions. The instructions are self-explanatory, and no previous experience is required to conduct this experiment. Carefully read through all the instructions beforehand, so that you are absolutely certain of each step in the experiment.

BACKGROUND   For years, entertainers have employed mnemon-
INFORMATION ic (memory) devices to thrill audiences with their great
feats of recollection. It is only recently, however, that
scientists have seriously explored the use of mnemonic
devices to facilitate or increase learning. The present experiment will demonstrate the usefulness of one such de-
vice, visual imagery. Basically, you will have two groups
of subjects trying to learn words in a given order. One
group of students will not be given any practice in the
use of visual imagery. The second group of students will
be given practice in the use of visual imagery as it applies
to the recollection of words. *It is predicted that the
group using visual imagery will be able to recall a greater
number of words.* As an added wrinkle, we shall see if
there is a difference between males and females in the
number of words remembered. We shall not make any
predictions on this point and leave it open as an exploratory question. (Obviously, those of you who are in a
non-coed setting will not bother with the comparison of
males and females.)

PROCEDURES: First, you will need to split the students into two
OVERVIEW   subject groups. You can do this by reading aloud a number that will be assigned to each student. The numbers
will range from one to the number of students in the
class. Students assigned odd numbers will constitute the
non-imagery group, while those given even numbers will
constitute the imagery group. Those given odd numbers
will be asked to turn to page 103, where they will read
instructions for learning the list without imagery. Likewise, those assigned even numbers will turn to page 105,
where they will read instructions for learning the list
with imagery. Subjects should be told to read only their
own instructions and not those given to their neighbors.
As the experimenter, you should read through the instructions to familiarize yourself with what each group
is expected to do.

Since we want each subject to be totally naive about what members of the other group are doing, you should defer all questions until the end of the experiment. Subjects should be given sufficient time to read the instructions.

After the subjects have finished reading their instructions, ask them to rip out a sheet of looseleaf paper on which they should number the horizontal lines from one to twenty. Later, they will use this paper to write down the words they can recall. Once this has been done you can read off the list of words on page 100 at ten-second intervals. It will be helpful to use a stopwatch, but a regular watch with a second hand will do. As a final note, you should bring along some pencils for those subjects who did not bring anything to write with.

After reading the list, ask the subjects to write down as many words as they can in their given order. Once this has been accomplished, subjects can turn to the scoring key on page 107, where they can find out how many words they correctly recalled. Subjects could then pass their sheets to the front of the room with the number of correct answers circled on top. You could list the scores on the blackboard and subjects could calculate the mean for each group using the format on page 109.

Explicit instructions follow below. The complete experiment should take no more than 40 minutes.

INSTRUCTIONS

1.   *Introduction—Assignment to Groups*
"We are about to begin our experiment. In order to properly conduct the experiment I shall need two groups of subjects. I shall point to each of you and read out a number starting with one. Remember your number. Those assigned odd numbers will be in group one, while those assigned even numbers will be in group two." (Proceed to assign the numbers.)

2.   *Subjects Read Instructions*

"Now that you know what group you are in, I would like people with the odd numbers to turn to page 103, where they can read the instructions for their group. The people with even numbers should turn to page 105, where they can read their instructions. Be sure to turn to the correct page. No questions will be answered during the experiment."

3.   *Preparing Papers for Scoring*

When everybody has finished reading his instructions, say the following: "Okay, now I'd like each of you to rip a page out of your notebook and number the lines downward from one to twenty. In addition, I'd like you to enter your assigned number on the upper left hand corner of the page. I'd also like you to write in an M if you are a male and an F if you are a female."

4.   *Reading the List*

Now you can prepare the subjects for the list. "I am going to read off a list of twenty words, and I'd like you to try to remember as many words as possible in the order in which they have been read. Do not write down any words until I give the order to do so."

Read the list with a ten-second pause after each word.

1. car	11. barn
2. flag	12. nail
3. clock	13. rat
4. knife	14. ball
5. shirt	15. lamp
6. drum	16. rug
7. scissors	17. apple
8. pen	18. telephone
9. ski	19. airplane
10. supper	20. pencil

5.   *Subject Scoring*

When you have read the list, allow two minutes for the subjects to write down as many words as possible. Subjects will write the words on the looseleaf paper. After two minutes, tell the subjects to stop and turn to the scoring key on page 107. They can then calculate the number of correct answers and place the total in the upper right hand corner of their sheet. Once this is done, the subjects can pass their papers to the front of the room.

6.   *Results*

Write on the board the number of words correctly scored for males and females of the visual and non-visual imagery groups. (You can tell which group a subject is in by the number in the upper right hand corner of his paper.) Table 4, on page 109, will show you how to organize the results. While you are doing this, the subjects can read through the experimental instructions to familiarize themselves with the experiment.

After this has been done, the subjects can turn to page 109 and compute the mean for each of the four groups (male imagery, female imagery, male non-imagery, female non-imagery.

7.   *Discussion*

You will probably find that the group using imagery recalls more words correctly. There probably will not be much of a difference found between males and females. You may wish to discuss these results. For example: What are the teaching implications if memory is found to increase learning? How can students use imagery to study more effectively?

You may also try to think of ideas for future studies. For example, what would happen if you gave subjects only a five-second interval between words? Would this interval be too short to improve their memory powers? What kind of study could be designed to answer this question?

ODD NUMBERS

Subject Instructions

Note: We are using two different sets of instructions in this experiment. Do not discuss this material with your neighbor since he or she will likely have the other form and such discussion will bias the data.

You are about to participate in a task that involves learning a series of twenty words in their proper order. Your teacher will read off a list of twenty words. You are to remember these words in the order in which they are read. For example, if the list were composed of *book, shoe, turkey, fork,* you would try to remember the words in order, i.e., *book, shoe, turkey, fork.* To help make this process clearer, take a minute to memorize the following words in their proper order: chair, bed, orange, child.

Do not write down any words unless instructed to do so by the teacher. No questions will be answered during the experiment, so follow the teacher's instructions carefully. The teacher will provide further information after everyone has finished reading the instructions.

DO NOT TURN PAGE UNLESS TOLD TO DO SO

EVEN NUMBERS

Subject Instructions

Note: We are using two different sets of instructions
in this experiment. Do not discuss this material with your
neighbor since he or she will likely have the other form
and such discussion will bias the data.

The teacher will read off a list of twenty words. Your
task is to learn these words in their proper order. To help
you do this, think of visual images linking consecutive words
—i.e., the first word with the second word, the second word
with the third word, the third with the fourth, the fourth
with the fifth, the fifth with the sixth, etc. Thus, if a list of
twenty words were composed of *book, shoe, turkey, fork,*
and twenty other words, you might conjure up images of a
book resting on a *shoe,* a *shoe* being worn by a *turkey,* a
piece of *turkey* meat being cut by a *fork,* a *fork* connected
by an image with the fifth word, the fifth word connected
by an image with the sixth word, the sixth word with the
seventh word, etc. You will later use these images to help
remember the words in their proper order, i.e., book, shoe,
turkey, fork, etc. To understand this method better, take a
minute to make images that link the following words: chair,
bed, orange, child.
Do not write down any words unless instructed to do
so by the teacher. No questions will be answered during the
experiment, so please follow the teacher's instructions carefully. The teacher will provide further information after
everyone has finished reading the instructions.

DO NOT TURN PAGE UNLESS TOLD TO DO SO

SCORING KEY

1. car	11. barn
2. flag	12. nail
3. clock	13. rat
4. knife	14. ball
5. shirt	15. lamp
6. drum	16. rug
7. scissors	17. apple
8. pen	18. telephone
9. ski	19. airplane
10. supper	20. pencil

SCORING RULES

To be correct, the word must be one of those indicated on the above list and must be listed in its correct order.

SCORING EXAMPLE

If the subject wrote down the following list: car, flag, clock, shirt, knife, horn, scissors he would receive a score of 4. Car, flag, clock, and scissors are all on the list, and they are in their proper list position of 1, 2, 3, and 7. Shirt and knife are wrong because they are not written down in the order in which they appeared on the list. On the original list, knife was fourth and shirt was fifth. Horn is also incorrect; it was not on the original list.

RESULTS SHEET

List the scores for the male imagery group in column 1, the female imagery group in column 2, the male non-imagery group in column 3, and the female non-imagery group in column 4. After you have done that, find the mean scores for each group (see page 51 of the statistics section) and write these scores in Table 5 below.

TABLE 4

Results

Even Numbers Males Imagery	Even Numbers Females Imagery	Odd Numbers Males Non-imagery	Odd Numbers Females Non-imagery

TABLE 5

Mean Number of Words Recalled

	Imagery	Non-imagery
Males		
Females		

DEVELOPING HYPOTHESES

The following is a list of exploratory questions about human behavior:

1. When people see a stranger in need of help, what will they do?
2. Does the color of your hair have anything to do with how much fun you get out of life?
3. If people are observed while they are working, does it affect their work in any way?
4. Will people who take big risks get a better result than people who take moderate or low risks?
5. How will lowering the speed limit affect highway fatalities?
6. Are there characteristic differences in the way men and women look at their fingernails?
7. If you wanted someone to lend you $10, would it make any difference if you had borrowed a small amount before?

Form small groups of students (four or five) on the basis of their interest in one of these topics. Each group should develop *several* specific predictions about an exploratory question using the criteria that each hypothesis they develop must be both testable and specific. Let's take as an example the exploratory question, "How does the amount of freedom a teacher permits students in deciding how a course should be run affect the students' satisfaction with that course?"

After a discussion of the issues, and especially after specifically thinking about what kinds of freedom a teacher could permit, you might come up with many hypotheses. Here are a few examples:

1. Students will be more satisfied in classes where there is more freedom.
2. Students with good academic records will be more satisfied in freer classes, but students with poor records will be less satisfied.
3. Students will be more satisfied in classes where they determine the topics for study, but less satisfied when they have to make up the exam questions.

After the hypotheses are developed (about 15 minutes) let each group present its hypotheses and let the other groups in the class react to them using the criterion: "Is this a *specific* and *testable* prediction?"

Note: Be careful not to get trapped into a debate about whether a hypothesis is correct or incorrect. That question must be answered by research. What should be discussed is whether good hypotheses were formulated.

INDIVIDUAL OR CLASS EXERCISE: DEVELOPING HYPOTHESES

Question: What makes a hypothesis a "hypothesis"?

Answer: 1. It is a statement of a specific relationship between two variables.
2. The predicted relationship can be measured.

Examples: Students who drink beer get better grades than students who drink coke.

or Teachers who spend time talking with students individually give higher grades than teachers who keep to themselves.

Below are three situations. Read each one and after you read it try to develop a specific idea or prediction about the relationship between two variables in the situation. (One way to begin is to list the variables in each situation first and then think about how they may be related.)

During the Korean War some American soldiers fell into the hands of the North Koreans and were kept in prison camps. Most were exposed to "brainwashing" which is a very serious attempt to persuade someone to change his ideas, his opinions, and his values. At the end of the war some soldiers returned to America while others refused to return saying they preferred to remain and renounced their country.

Hint: How are people changed, what processes? What kinds of people are most susceptible to brainwashing?

A lady coming out of the grocery store with two heavy sacks drops one of the sacks and groceries go rolling everywhere. Four or five people are coming into the store at the same time, they pass the lady but do not stop. Three or four minutes later one person coming into the store sees the lady picking up cans and stops to help.

Hint: When do people stop to help? Does the presence or absence of other people affect how likely they are to help?

Two families in New York have different policies in their families for watching TV. In Family A children can only watch programs that have no violence, in Family B children can watch anything they want but they can only watch one hour of TV on school nights. Both families believe that TV affects their children. What might some of the effect be?

TESTING A HYPOTHESIS

Take as a hypothesis: Students who are high participators in class discussions are better liked by fellow classmates than students who are low participators.

Break the class into small groups, each of which has the task of making a plan for testing the hypothesis above. Each plan presented should be able to answer the following questions:

1. How can you determine who is a high and who is a low participator in class discussions?
2. How is "liking" operationalized and measured?
3. What are the steps in the research design?
4. How can you tell if the hypothesis is supported or not?

After each group has developed a plan, it should be presented to the entire class. The students then select the best plan and use it either in that class period or in the next period to test the hypothesis in their own or another class. (Note: This last step, actually using the plan to test the hypothesis, is optional. The exercise may still be used without actually testing the plans developed.)

SELECTING A METHOD
AND DEVELOPING A DESIGN

Assume that we are interested in knowing whether or not people will help other people. Our hypothesis is: People are more likely to help strangers when others are not present than when there are other people present. How can we test this prediction?

ACTIVITY 1

Break the class into small groups of four or five students. Using the hypothesis above, have one group develop an experiment to test it, one group a survey, one group an observational study. If there are more than three groups, repeat the assignments. Have groups refer to this manual for material appropriate to the method they will use.

When the groups have finished their designs, compare them in a class discussion. Which seems to be the best method for testing this particular hypothesis? Does more than one method look workable? What are the advantages and disadvantages of each method? If you find that it is possible to conduct a good experiment, a good survey, and a good observational study, do not be surprised. There is no right method; each can be used successfully. However, you will probably find that each method provides a slightly different answer. A survey might tell you what people *think* they might do or what they remember doing. An experiment might give you an idea of what people will do under a specific set of circumstances. An observational study might tell you how people act in different places.

ACTIVITY 2

Activity 1 can be done partly as an out-of-class activity. As a homework assignment, ask students individually (or in groups if they can meet out of class) to develop a plan for testing the hypothesis, making sure that several students are assigned to each method. In class, have students with the same method compare what they have done out of class and report it to the whole class. Then the entire class can engage in the discussion described above.

Note to teachers: You can do either of these activities using a hypothesis developed by the students in your class.

DIFFERENT TYPES OF QUESTIONS GIVE DIFFERENT INFORMATION

There is almost always more than one way to ask for information. The way you ask for information in part determines the kind of information you get back. For that reason, it is important that you think carefully before writing questions. With regard to the demonstration questions below, you will probably find that smokers and non-smokers do not answer the first question differently. However, there will probably be a difference in the way the two groups answer question 2. The following exercise illustrates these points. Go through the steps indicated below and see what conclusions you reach. It is advisable that there be at least five smokers in the class for you to undertake this activity.

1. Have everyone in the class answer the three questions in the survey below:

   a. Do you think that smoking leads to lung cancer?
      ____YES ____NO
   b. In your opinion, what is the probability (0% to 100%) that smoking will lead to lung cancer?
      _____%
   c. Do you smoke? ____YES ____NO

2. Collect the data. Tabulate questions *a* and *b* for the whole class. Find the percentage of YES's and NO's for question *a* and the average (mean) for question *b*. Compare the results. Do you get the same kind of information from each question? What are the differences? When might you prefer one kind or the other?

3. Now divide the data into two piles, those who answer YES to question c and those who answer NO. Retabulate the data for questions a and b for smokers and non-smokers. Compare the data for the two groups for question a. Are there differences? How do you interpret them? Compare the data for the two groups for question b, and note any differences that might occur. How do you interpret the results?

TO THE TEACHER

This research guide has been prepared as a supplement to regular texts for high school courses in Psychology, Social Science, Sociology, Anthropology, and Political Science. We suggest that there are several ways to use it:

1. As a step-by-step guide for a class research project. Projects of this nature can be done in class in an intensive unit of several weeks or at a more leisurely pace over the whole semester.

2. As a teaching unit about research in which the guide is assigned as required reading and the activities in the text and at the end are used as teaching aids to illustrate and enliven the material.

3. As a guide for an individual student's independent study or honors project.

This guide is divided into three sections. In the main body of the text we describe and illustrate the basic steps in research. Where it seems useful we have included some additional references which could be of help to students who wish to go further or to teachers in preparing supplementary material for class presentation. After the basic material two longer examples of research projects are given. One is a survey and the other an experiment. The presentation of each piece of research is organized to follow the steps in the guide. Finally, there is a section of activities which can be completed in a class period or less time. They will permit students to experience some of the steps described in the first section in more depth.

This guide was first prepared for a high school social science project with which we became involved several years ago. The enthusiasm of students for investigating an issue or idea that they found interesting has led us to believe that this expanded version could be a real asset to student research projects. Several of the students who reviewed a prepublication manuscript of this guide* indicated they wished they could have read it before doing projects they had undertaken. We want to express our appreciation especially to the two social science teachers who have worked closely with us throughout this project and whose thoughtful comments are incorporated in this guide, Mr. Paul Pascoe of Kenmore West High School, in Kenmore, N.Y. and Mr. Robert Heffern of Maryvale High School in Cheektowaga, N.Y.

*We are grateful to the following high school students who read and commented on an earlier version of this manuscript: Mary Eldridge, John Godard, Tom Hart, and Ann Victor.